The Impact of Labor Taxes on Labor Supply

To my wife, Ninette, for her love and support.

The Impact of Labor Taxes on Labor Supply

An International Perspective

Richard Rogerson

The AEI Press

Publisher for the American Enterprise Institute

WASHINGTON, D.C.

Distributed by arrangement with the Rowman & Littlefield Publishing Group, 4501 Forbes Boulevard, Suite 200, Lanham, Maryland 20706. To order call toll free 1-800-462-6420 or 1-717-794-3800. For all other inquiries please contact AEI Press, 1150 Seventeenth Street, N.W. Washington, D.C. 20036 or call 1-800-862-5801.

This publication is a project of the National Research Initiative, a program of the American Enterprise Institute that is designed to support, publish, and disseminate research by university-based scholars and other independent researchers who are engaged in the exploration of important public policy issues.

Library of Congress Cataloging-in-Publication Data

Rogerson, Richard Donald.
    The impact of labor taxes on labor supply : an international
perspective / Richard Rogerson.
    p. cm.
  Includes bibliographical references.
    ISBN-13: 978-0-8447-4355-4 (cloth)
    ISBN-10: 0-8447-4355-0 (cloth)
    ISBN-13: 978-0-8447-4356-1 (pbk.)
    ISBN-10: 0-8447-4356-9 (pbk.)
    [etc.]
  1. Labor supply. 2. Taxation. 3. Fiscal policy. 4. Labor economics. I. Title.

HD5706.R64 2010
331.1—dc22

                                                2010009574

14 13 12 11 10   1 2 3 4 5

Printed in the United States of America

Contents

List of Illustrations

Figures

Tables

Preface

The research that serves as the foundation for this monograph has occupied a great deal of my research time for much of the last ten years. The original motivation for this research was the simple observation that there are dramatic differences in time devoted to market work across rich industrialized countries, and that these differences have emerged over the last fifty years. Having documented these large differences and the timing of their appearance, I then undertook the task of trying to understand what factors might account for them. The list of potential explanations was a long one, but my conclusion is that differences in the scale of tax and transfer systems are most likely the dominant factor behind the large differences in time devoted to market work.

This conclusion has important implications for policymakers. In particular, it implies that when policymakers are considering increases to the scale of tax and transfer systems, they must recognize that these increases entail an important cost: the lost output associated with reduced work effort. This case is presented in the academic papers that I and my coauthors have written over the last ten years. The goal of this monograph is to summarize this case in a transparent fashion. I believe this summary is particularly important precisely because many policymakers fail to recognize this evidence.

In the course of my research I have had the pleasure and good fortune to work with many individuals who have greatly contributed to my understanding of the issues I address. This list includes Jorge Alonso-Ortiz, Lei Fang, Hugo Hopenhayn, Per Krusell, Cara McDaniel, Ellen McGrattan, Toshi Mukoyama, Lee Ohanian, Edward Prescott, Michael Pries, Andrea Raffo, Aysegul Sahin, Robert Shimer, Johanna Wallenius, and Randall Wright. I have also benefited from comments by and discussions with many other individuals. They are too numerous to list here, but they too helped shape this work.

I would particularly like to thank two people who were especially important in my decision to write this monograph: Steve Davis of the University of Chicago and the American Enterprise Institute, and Henry Olsen of the American Enterprise Institute. Steve had seen my work and urged me to present it to a broader audience beyond academic economists, and he arranged for me to present some of my work on labor taxes and hours of work at the American Enterprise Institute in the spring of 2007. Henry Olsen subsequently contacted me about the possibility of making my work available to a broader policy audience, and from there we decided to go ahead with this monograph. I would like to thank Henry for this opportunity to publish my findings, as well as for helpful comments on earlier drafts. I would also like to thank Emily Batman at AEI for her useful comments on earlier drafts of this monograph, and Anne Himmelfarb for her help with editing.

Introduction

High levels of government expenditure are a pervasive feature of all modern industrialized economies. In 2006, total government expenditures as a fraction of gross domestic product (GDP) averaged more than 40 percent in countries belonging to the Organisation for Economic Cooperation and Development (OECD).[1] In several countries, including France, Italy, and Sweden, this ratio exceeded 50 percent. Although this fraction is lower in the United States than in most other advanced economies, even here it exceeded 35 percent. Government spending funds many different programs and activities, including entitlement programs such as Social Security and Medicare, social insurance programs such as unemployment insurance and disability insurance, and services such as health care, education, and national defense. An important public policy issue in all economies is to determine the scale at which these programs should be operated. These permanent or long-run decisions about government policy play a significant role in defining the overall economic climate of the United States and thus have a large influence on the long-run economic well-being of Americans.

The United States faces important decisions about the size of its government spending programs. Pressure for change comes in part from the budgetary imbalances associated with changing demographics—the aging of the baby boomers and increasing life expectancies—as well as from the increasing relative cost of health care. Effective public policy decisions about the longer-run scale of various government programs require a careful assessment of both the costs and benefits associated with the size of these programs and the manner in which they are funded. This monograph focuses on the costs associated with these programs. Central to understanding these costs is the fact that the revenues funding government programs are raised largely by taxes on labor. It follows that an unfortunate and unintended consequence of expanded government spending is a disincentive for individuals to work. Because labor is the dominant input used in producing output, less labor implies less output, which in turn means that overall consumption and living standards must decrease. Or, as some commentators put it, expanding the size of government programs shrinks the size of the pie that everyone must share.

But how large is this disincentive effect? Is it of first-order importance for policymakers, or can it safely be ignored? Many policymakers seem to believe that the effect is small and can therefore be ignored. In this monograph I present evidence suggesting that this belief is seriously mistaken. The belief that disincentive effects are small tends to be based on studies using unreliable methods applied to U.S. data. I argue that the most valuable and reliable information about these disincentive effects is found outside of the United States.

To appreciate why it is important to look abroad for evidence on these effects, it is important to first understand why the United States is not a good source of evidence, and why many policymakers are drawing unwarranted conclusions from U.S. data. Because there have been changes in the scale and design of government spending in the United States over the last fifty or so years, in principle the historical data could tell us about the magnitude of the effects of labor taxes on hours of work. But certain realities serve to obscure these disincentive effects in the U.S. data. Central among them is that the changes in U.S. programs over the last fifty years have not been particularly large, and that many other changes have also affected the economy during this time. When many changes occur simultaneously, it is difficult to reliably determine the contribution of any one particular factor to the overall economic changes that we observe. Some would say that we have a situation where the signal-to-noise ratio is relatively small.

Failure to appreciate this fact has led some observers to argue that higher taxes on labor do not lead people to work less. In the context of recent debates about the economy, several policymakers have observed that labor taxes increased during the 1990s, but that total hours of work in the U.S. economy nonetheless grew substantially. This is proposed as evidence that higher taxes do not create a disincentive for work. But this argument neglects to take into account that something else very substantial was also affecting the U.S. economy at this time. In particular, the 1990s were characterized by high investment levels, high productivity growth, and high output growth. (Some proclaimed the advent of a "New Economy.") It is hardly surprising that total hours of work increased during a period featuring an investment boom and high productivity growth. No one suggests that the high rate of investment and high productivity growth were due to the increase in taxes; that is, they are thought to be the result of other factors. It follows that economic outcomes in general in this period, including hours worked, were probably dominated by these other factors. In short, this episode provides no information about the disincentive effects of higher labor taxes.

In the monograph I will explain in detail why the United States is not a good source of information about these disincentive effects. I will also explain why a second source of information on disincentive effects, the large literature in the field of labor economics, is problematic. This literature studies data on the choices made by individual American workers in different situations to infer how they would respond to changes in tax and transfer programs. Much of it concludes that the overall disincentive effects of higher taxes are relatively small. But we need to understand that the immediate findings of this research are typically very sensitive to the specifications used in the analyses and that the conclusions regarding the disincentive effects for the overall economy come from making extrapolations that are not justified by the analyses. Unfortunately, many policymakers continue to base their analysis on these estimates.

So why should we turn to the experiences of other countries for evidence? As I describe in detail later on, the most transparent source of information would come from a situation where large permanent changes in the scale of tax and transfer programs have occurred, where these changes were large compared to other changes in the economy over the same period, and where there has been sufficient time for individuals to respond to the changes. While the United States does not fit this ideal situation, it turns out that these three conditions are much more likely to be met in some other advanced economies.

A striking feature of the evolution of labor taxes in other advanced economies is that there have been very dramatic differences across countries in the extent to which these taxes have changed over time. For example, since 1960, taxes on labor in some European countries have increased by more than three times as much as in the United States. Moreover, the majority of these changes occurred prior to 1980, so that sufficient time has evolved for individuals to adjust their behavior. It follows that looking at the changes in hours worked and labor taxes across OECD countries provides an excellent opportunity to learn about the disincentive effects of labor taxes.

The patterns in the data from other countries are striking. Consider two large European economies, those of France and Germany. In these two countries, total hours of work relative to population are roughly 30 percent less than in the United States. At the same time, taxes on labor are about twenty percentage points higher. But most remarkable is the fact that fifty years ago, both the differences in taxes and the differences in hours of work were much smaller. Whereas some analysts seem to think that Europe has always been different from the United States in terms of both the size of government and the amount that people work, the data show quite clearly that this is not the case. The relative increase in the size of government and the relative decrease in the amount of work that people do are both changes that have occurred since 1960.

Over time, countries such as France and Germany have steadily and consistently increased taxes on labor relative to the United States, at the same time that hours of work have steadily and consistently decreased relative to the United States. These data are the basis for the estimated magnitude of the disincentive effects that I provide. I estimate that a 10-percentage-point increase in labor taxes used to fund transfer programs leads to a reduction in hours worked of between ten and fifteen percentage points. I conclude that these disincentive effects are large and that they therefore need to be taken into account by policymakers considering long-run reforms to government spending programs. In view of their importance, it is very unfortunate that so many policymakers continue to neglect them.

While I have thus far described the issue that will be the focus of this monograph, I note two issues it will not address. I stress that their absence does not suggest that they are not important. One prominent issue in current discussions regarding tax reform concerns the distribution of the tax burden. Recent proposals have called for tax increases on "rich" households, with different proposals offering different definitions of "rich."

Assessing the consequences of such proposals is important, but is not something that I attempt here. Instead, my goal is to bring attention to the fact that tax and transfer programs have large effects on overall labor supply. While the issue of how this decrease in labor supply is distributed across different groups is also important, my primary goal is to establish the importance of the effects of labor taxes on total labor supply.

Second, given the recent focus on the impact and desirability of different stimulus policies adopted by the government, it is important to emphasize that this monograph is about the consequences of long-run or permanent features of the tax and transfer system. It is not about the short-term effects of temporary changes in various economic policies, which—especially when enacted in unusual circumstances—can be very different from the longer-run effects of permanent changes in policies. Thus the effects that I discuss in this monograph should not be interpreted as bearing directly on the likely effects of the various stimulus measures involving changes in taxes and government spending, or short-term deficit-financed government spending.

The remainder of the introduction summarizes the chapters that follow. Chapter 1 presents the key ideas from economic theory that will serve as the foundation for the subsequent analysis. It begins with a simple model of labor supply in the presence of a government that operates a tax and transfer system. Like standard textbook treatments, this model assumes that a household derives utility from consumption and leisure, and that the key decision that it faces is how to divide its time between leisure and working, thereby trading off between leisure time and the level of consumption.

Several important results are derived from this model. First, the effect of labor taxes on labor supply depends crucially on what the government does with the resulting tax revenue. If the government uses the funds to finance a transfer program (such as Medicare), there will be a negative effect on labor supply. The logic of this result is simple: people work so that they can afford things that they desire. If the government provides these things free of charge, then there is less incentive to work. On the other hand, if the government uses the funds for wasteful activities, say to hire workers who provide no services valued by consumers, then there will be no effect on aggregate hours worked. Loosely speaking, although the taxes that the government levies lead people to supply fewer hours of work, these are completely offset by the hours of government employees. A third case is that the government uses the tax revenues to subsidize consumption, an example being subsidies to child care. In this case there is also no overall effect on labor supply. While the higher taxes discourage consumption and encourage leisure, leading to less work, the subsidy to consumption has the opposite effects, thereby offsetting the initial decrease in work.

The second important point concerns the relationship between the social cost of government spending programs and the effect of taxes on labor supply. Specifically, even though wasteful government spending does not lead to an overall decrease in work, it does entail a social cost, because the fact that some workers are not producing anything of value means the output is lower than it otherwise would be. In the case of a transfer program, resources are not wasted in this same sense, but the decrease in labor supply once again means that less output is being produced. In the case of a subsidy to consumption, there is no effect on labor supply and no social cost—the subsidy to consumption effectively undoes the negative effects of the tax on labor. It follows that one should not equate the labor supply effects of taxes with the social cost of taxation, since the relationship between the two is apparently more complicated.

A third important result is that taxes on labor income, payroll (paid by both the worker and the employer), and consumption all represent taxes on labor. Although a tax on consumption may seem distinct from a tax on labor, consumption taxes serve to distort the rate at which individual workers can trade off leisure time for consumption, just as a tax on labor income does.

Chapter 2 discusses in more detail the issue of where we should look for evidence regarding the disincentive effects of labor taxes. The key message here is that the ideal data will be from countries that instituted large permanent changes in labor taxes sufficiently long ago for the effects to be visible.

Chapters 3 and 4 take a closer look at what we can learn from the U.S. economic data in the last fifty years. Chapter 3 describes the evolution of labor taxes, government spending, and total hours of work in the United States since 1956. Chapter 4 then looks at what these data have to tell us. There are two main findings that I emphasize. First, the United States is not an ideal case study. Changes in taxes here have not been very large, so other changes during this time period are at least as important as the changes in taxes. One cannot infer the pure effect of taxes from a simple look at the data. Instead, one needs to properly control for the other changes that are going on in addition to changes in labor taxes. It is the failure to control for these other changes that lead to the mistaken conclusion that labor taxes have little effect on hours of work.

The most significant change that must be controlled for is the dramatic increase in female labor force participation. I describe in chapter 4 how this effect might be removed from the data. To do this in a systematic manner requires a framework that is somewhat richer than that introduced in chapter 1. Specifically, it requires the explicit incorporation of the concept economists refer to as "home production." This term reminds us that many service activities can either be performed by the individual or purchased in the market. Important examples are meal preparation and child care. Incorporating home production is critical in understanding the evolution of market work in the United States in the last fifty years, because one of the key changes associated with the entry of women into the labor force during this period is that time devoted to home production has decreased significantly. At the same time, both leisure time and market work have increased somewhat. A framework that considers market work and leisure as the only two uses of time would necessarily be unable to reconcile these two increases.

To understand the movement from home production to market production—broadly synonymous with the large movement of women into the labor force—one must allow for some force that moves the economy in this direction, be it technological advancements in home production (e.g., appliances such as washing machines, dryers, and microwaves, or greater availability and quality of prepared foods), or changes in social norms regarding the role of women. A key point is that such a force must be recognized as another important force shaping market work in addition to those that are associated with changes in taxes. It turns out that this force is sufficiently large that it dominates the relatively small change in labor taxes that occurred in the United States.

The second key result in chapter 4 is that after controlling for this key trend (based on changes in time devoted to home production), I find that the U.S. data show large disincentive effects of labor taxes on work: a ten percentage point increase in taxes leads to a decrease in hours worked of between 10 and 15 percent.

In my view, the disincentive effects are indeed present in the U.S. data. Some may nonetheless remain skeptical that this is so, since in order to find the effects it is necessary to implement controls for the underlying forces driving female labor force participation, which are not yet completely understood. It is precisely because of this that the evidence from other countries is so important. Even though the movement of women into the labor force is occurring in other countries as well as in the United States, the large changes in taxes outside the United States allow us to observe the effects of taxes on market work in a more transparent fashion. Moreover, because increases in taxes create an opposing force to the one that is leading more women to work in the market, countries with larger increases in tax rates will therefore tend to have smaller effects associated with this additional force.

Chapter 5 presents the main empirical findings of the cross-country analysis. I begin with a simple presentation of the trends in hours worked among OECD countries since 1960, which leads to a striking observation. Namely, changes in hours of market work since 1960 have varied tremendously across countries. At one extreme are countries such as the United States, Australia, and Canada, which have seen either relatively little change or modest increases in hours of market work. At the other extreme are countries such as France and Germany, which have seen declines in hours of market work that exceed 35 percent. The average across all countries shows a decrease of almost 20 percent.

I then examine the evolution of labor taxes across these same countries. The average labor tax increased over this period from 25 percent to more than 40 percent. The relationship between the change in labor taxes and the change in hours of work in each country confirms that changes in labor taxes are indeed a key factor in accounting for the large differences in trend changes in hours worked across countries. Specifically, the results indicate that a ten percentage point increase in labor taxes leads to a decrease in overall hours worked in the economy of more than 10 percent.

Chapter 5 goes on to examine the extent to which there are other explanations for the relative decline in hours of work in many European countries. I find that neither the prevalence of unions nor labor market regulation can explain the large decline in work in Europe. I also consider the possibility that Europeans have different attitudes about work than Americans, or value leisure more, and I describe why these explanations do not seem compelling.

While chapter 5 presents strong evidence that an increase in labor taxes has a substantial negative effect on market work, I also acknowledge that some countries do not at first glance fit this pattern. In particular, any argument about the negative effects of taxes on hours of market work faces an apparently serious challenge from the Scandinavian countries. Scandinavian governments are at least as large as others in continental Europe; yet hours worked in Scandinavia are substantially higher.

The key to reconciling these observations is the result from chapter 1 concerning the nature of government spending. A distinctive feature of Scandinavian government spending is that, relative to spending by other European governments, a much larger share goes for government employment and government programs (such as child care and elderly care). By using tax revenues to subsidize these services, the government serves to undo the direct effects of taxes, and thereby lessen the negative effects on market work. Chapter 6 presents this argument.

Chapter 7 concludes the monograph and discusses the relevance of these findings for current policy discussions in the United States.

As this summary suggests, this monograph will cover a fair bit of territory and will discuss many subtle points raised by specific findings. For the reader looking for a single bottom line from this analysis, I point to the finding that a ten percentage point increase in labor taxes reduces hours worked by between 10 and 15 percent. In other words, the disincentive effects of labor taxes are large. For example, if paying for the various plans proposed by the Obama administration requires a 5 percent increase in tax rates on labor, the result will be a decrease in hours of work of 5 percent or more. In terms of the lost output, this amounts to something equivalent to a serious recession. But whereas recessions are temporary, the implied reduction in this case would be permanent.

1

Labor Taxes and Hours of Work: Some Theory

The idea that higher taxes on labor discourage individuals from working is one that most people would accept without the need for economic theory. Of greater interest is the magnitude of this disincentive effect, which many would argue is an empirical issue, not a theoretical issue. Nonetheless, in this chapter I show that basic economic theory plays an essential role in the effort to understand the magnitude of this effect by helping us understand how to interpret the data properly.

Specifically, theory helps us to understand why, perhaps contrary to intuition, not all tax increases on labor are the same. In order to predict how taxes on labor affect the labor supply decisions of individuals, I will argue, one also has to know how the government will use the revenues that it receives from the labor taxes. This contention will be very relevant when we look to interpret the cross-country evidence on labor taxes and hours of work in a later chapter, and will help us understand why some analysts have mistakenly interpreted the data to imply that the effects of tax changes on labor supply are small.

The discussion in this chapter will also help to clarify which sets of taxes are relevant in assessing the total tax on labor. I will show that it is not only labor income taxes that matter, but also payroll taxes levied on employers and taxes on consumption. From the perspective of discouraging work, taxes on consumption, such as value-added taxes or sales taxes, act just like taxes on labor income. And in the case of payroll taxes, such as Social Security and Medicare taxes in the United States, both the employer and employee contributions matter.

There is one final benefit to presenting a theoretical framework in this chapter. This theory highlights how changes in labor taxes influence the economic decisions made by individuals. Any argument about how an economic policy affects economic outcomes should be based on an understanding of how and why the policy will affect the decisions that individuals make. The public should not allow policymakers to make claims about the effects of policies without articulating the manner in which these policies influence individual economic decisions.

The theoretical model used in this chapter is what economists think of as the canonical model of labor supply. I begin by describing this model and explain why it is useful for thinking about labor supply in the real world, despite its apparent simplicity. I show how this simple model can be used to analyze the effect of changes in tax policy on the total amount of work done in the economy. Although I introduce some notation to formalize the discussion and state results more clearly, the body of this chapter presents only the results along with some intuition. The ideas are developed more rigorously and in more detail in the appendix.

The Textbook Model of Labor Supply

The canonical model of labor supply can be found in any undergraduate textbook on labor economics. At the core of this model is the assumption that individuals value two things: consumption and leisure. Unfortunately, these two desires are in conflict with each other. Hence the decision that an individual makes about how much time to devote to work is really about the trade-off between consumption and leisure. More leisure implies less income and therefore less consumption, and conversely, less leisure implies more income and more consumption. The key to determining how tax policy influences the amount of work carried out in an economy is to first understand the trade-off that an individual faces between consumption and leisure, and then to assess how taxes affect this trade-off.

In order to have a clearer picture of this framework, it is useful to begin by formalizing the individual's decision about how much to work. Let c denote consumption, and h denote time devoted to work. It is convenient to think of the time devoted to work as a fraction of the individual's total time. The fraction of time devoted to leisure is then given by $1-h$.

A critical piece of information is how the individual feels about different combinations of consumption and leisure. We represent the preferences of the individual by the utility function $u(c, 1-h)$. Different people will prefer different combinations of consumption and leisure, but we can describe any individual's preferences with such a function.

The choices people end up making typically depend not only on their preferences but also on their opportunities. We think about an individual's opportunities in the following way: the individual faces a wage rate w per unit of time and a price of consumption equal to p, and he must decide how much time to devote to work. We also assume that this individual has some income or wealth in addition to income that is earned by working. We denote this amount of income by I. For most individuals, income from working is the main source of income, but there are some individuals who have substantial amounts of income that are not the result of work.[1]

The virtue of this model is that it allows us to capture in a simple and transparent setting some very basic economic forces that are fundamental to thinking about labor supply. This is why it remains the cornerstone of analyses of labor supply in undergraduate textbooks. To be sure, the results that we derive below can also be obtained in much more complex settings that might seem more realistic, though the analysis becomes more involved and more demanding technically.

Before we use this model of labor supply to derive any results, it is instructive to discuss some of the simplifying assumptions implicit in this framework, and how we should use the model to interpret the choices individuals make in the real world. First, this model assumes that there is a single consumption good. In reality, there are many different consumption goods, and an important decision is how to divide one's budget among them. It is straightforward to extend the analysis to allow for this, and none of the results is affected.

Second, this model assumes that all labor income must be spent on consumption, so that there is no decision about savings, and no option to (even temporarily) finance consumption by borrowing. In order to incorporate saving and borrowing, we would need to have a dynamic model, that is, a model in which there is more than one time period, and the individual would be making decisions that have a dynamic component. While models that consider the choices of individuals over their lifetime are very common in the economics literature, they are necessarily more complex and require greater mastery of some mathematical techniques. One benefit of considering dynamic models is that they allow the researcher to confront a larger set of issues. But the key observation from our perspective is that a dynamic model still necessarily involves the same key trade-off that our model captures: if individuals devote more time to work over their lifetime, then they can afford more consumption over their lifetime as well. In what follows we will interpret the time frame to be the individual's lifetime, so that the simple model just described can be interpreted as capturing the decision about how much to work over one's lifetime.

Third, this model assumes that individuals can choose how much they want to work at the going wage rate w, but in reality many jobs involve a specified number of hours. This observation does not constitute a fundamental critique of the simple model, however. To the extent that different occupations are associated with different levels of work, individuals with different preferences regarding leisure and consumption will presumably make different occupational choices. Also, in many situations an individual can choose between full-time and part-time work, and individuals who want to work additional hours can take a second job. Moreover, individuals still exercise choice about how much time to devote to work by deciding when to enter the labor force and when to retire. While there are many distinct margins that may be relevant, the key trade-off is still more lifetime leisure versus more lifetime consumption. A final point to note in this context is that even if jobs come with specified hours, employers who compete for workers have an incentive to take worker preferences into account when setting their workweeks. It follows that if some underlying economic force leads all individuals to want to work fewer hours, then employers will feel pressure to accommodate this. In this regard it is worth noting that prior to World War II, the standard workweek in manufacturing in the United States declined from over sixty hours per week to its current level of around forty hours per week. Most economists interpret this to reflect changes in the desired hours of work for individuals.

Fourth, this model considers the choice of a particular individual, whereas in reality most individuals are part of multimember households in which the choices of the individuals jointly determine the household's possibilities. While one can extend the simple model to allow for multimember households, it is true that each household nonetheless faces the same key trade-off captured above. That is, the more time that a household devotes to market work, the more consumption the household can afford.

Fifth, the model that I have described contains no uncertainty. In reality, how much individuals work during their lifetime may be heavily influenced by events that cannot be predicted in advance, such as illness or unanticipated opportunities. While these events are very important in shaping the outcomes for a particular household, they are not so important in analyzing the whole economy, because they tend to average out across individuals.

To summarize, one can construct much more complicated models of labor supply than the simple textbook model. These models allow for a richer set of issues to be addressed, and appear more realistic. But ultimately, all still assume that a basic trade-off exists between leisure time and consumption. In what follows, the reader should view the simple model from the perspective of a household that is deciding how much time to devote to work over its lifetime. The conclusions that I draw in the remainder of this chapter are the result of analyzing how tax policy interacts with this trade-off, and are applicable even if the model is extended to allow for many additional features.

A Diagrammatic Representation of the Consumption-Leisure Trade-Off

It is instructive to examine the implicit trade-off between consumption and leisure more closely. A key point is that the perceived terms of this trade-off change as the individual varies his or her hours of work. This is because when consumption is low and leisure is high, an individual tends to value additional consumption a lot and does not value additional leisure so highly. This is a basic feature of preferences: the more of any good that an individual consumes, the less valuable is an additional unit of that good. Or, put somewhat differently, and in the context of our situation, if an individual has lots of spare time, then additional spare time may not be so valuable, but when an individual has very little spare time, then additional spare time is quite valuable.

Thus when an individual contemplates relatively high leisure (i.e., low hours of work) and hence low consumption, the benefit of additional leisure is relatively low, while the benefit of additional consumption is relatively high. In contrast, when consumption is high and leisure is low, the reverse is true: additional consumption is not very valuable but additional leisure is very valuable. This implies that at very high hours of work the benefits of additional hours are less than the cost, while at very low hours of work the reverse is true. Intuitively, this tells us that the worker's utility as a function of hours of work has the shape shown in figure 1-1. It is important to emphasize that this figure shows the trade-off facing one particular individual. Although all individuals must trade off between consumption and leisure, the exact trade-offs that they face and how they feel about them will vary from individual to individual, since individuals may have different preferences and face different wage rates.

FIGURE 1-1
THE LEISURE-CONSUMPTION TRADE-OFF

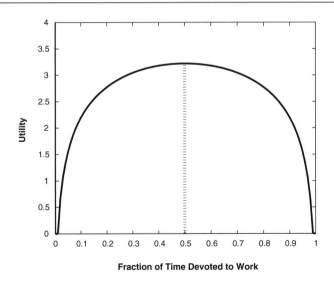

Fraction of Time Devoted to Work

SOURCE: Author's illustration.

At low levels of hours of work the individual consumes very little and has lots of leisure time, and as a result would benefit by giving up some leisure time in order to work more and afford more consumption. As this process continues, the increase in utility occurs at a decreasing rate, since the additional consumption becomes less valuable and the leisure time that is being sacrificed starts to become more valuable. At some point (at $h = .5$ in the figure), the situation reverses itself and the additional consumption is not sufficiently valuable to offset the loss in leisure time. Continuing beyond this point makes the individual progressively worse off. The optimal level of hours of work corresponds to the point at which this curve reaches its maximum. In the above figure this occurs when $h = .5$.

Income and Substitution Effects

In undergraduate textbooks, one of the basic messages about labor supply is that an increase in the wage (holding all else constant) has two opposing effects on desired hours of work. On the one hand, an increase in the wage makes individuals wealthier, because the same number of hours of work results in more income. When individuals become wealthier, they tend to consume more of the things that they enjoy, and as a result they increase both consumption and leisure. This is known as the wealth or income effect.

On the other hand, an increase in the wage also changes the rate at which individuals can trade leisure for consumption. In particular, if the wage increases, then each unit of leisure becomes more expensive in terms of the consumption that is sacrificed by working one less unit of time. When one good becomes more expensive relative to another good, the effect is to substitute the less expensive good for the more expensive good, and as a result, the individual decreases the amount of leisure and hence increases the time devoted to work. This is known as the substitution effect.

The reader should be able to recognize these competing forces associated with a wage increase. On the one hand, it now takes less work to maintain one's standard of living, but on the other hand, there is now a greater reward for sacrificing that last hour of leisure time.

It is useful to think of the income and substitution effects in a slightly different context. Suppose that instead of choosing between leisure and consumption, an individual is deciding how much of two different goods to buy. In this context, the income effect reflects the fact that if the individual's income goes up, he or she tends to buy more of all of the things that he or she likes. This may result in more consumption of restaurant meals, for example, and greater consumption of housing. The substitution effect reflects the fact that when the price of one good changes relative to that of the other, individuals tend to substitute the less expensive good for the more expensive good. When the price of gasoline goes up, both effects are present: the higher price of gasoline makes individuals feel poorer, thereby leading them to decrease consumption of all goods. But it also makes gasoline more expensive relative to other goods, so individuals also try to economize on gasoline relative to other purchases.

The same intuition applies to the case of an individual making a labor supply decision in the presence of a change in the wage rate. Combining the income and substitution effects, we see that in general, the effect of an increase in the wage rate on desired labor supply is ambiguous: the income effect tends to reduce desired labor supply, whereas the substitution effect tends to increase desired labor supply. Whether labor supply increases or decreases would therefore depend on the relative magnitude of the two effects, which is another way of saying that it depends on the exact form of the utility function.

However, a simple and powerful observation has proven to be very useful in providing information about preferences for an "average" individual. Specifically, if we look at what has happened on average in the United States since World War II, we see that the average time devoted to work by Americans has changed relatively little, while the average wage rate adjusted for inflation has more than doubled.

To see why this is an important piece of information, note that if a very large increase in wages leads to effectively no change in hours of work, then on average, income and substitution effects are roughly offsetting. It turns out that only a small set of utility functions satisfies this property, and knowing that this property holds allows us to maker sharper predictions about how labor supply responds to changes in taxes. The results that I describe below will assume that income and substitution effects offset each other. It is important to emphasize here that this result holds for the average individual. As noted above, in reality we know that different people have different preferences, so that for some the income effect may be larger, while for others the substitution effect may be larger. But the fact that Americans' wages overall have gone up but their hours worked have remained roughly constant implies that on average, the two effects are offsetting. Because the focus of this monograph is on what will happen to overall hours of work in the economy, this information is sufficient for our purposes.

Analyzing Tax Policy

The above discussion assumed that there was a single individual who was deciding how much to work and implicitly, therefore, how much to consume. The issue that I want to address here has to do with how taxes affect the amount of work done not just by one individual, but in the economy as a whole.

Let us consider a situation in which there are many individuals in the economy, which we denote by N, each of whom makes a decision about how much to work. We also assume that there are firms that hire workers to produce output. We next introduce a government into this framework and assess the effect of government's decisions about taxing and spending on economy-wide hours of work. On the revenue side, we assume that the government levies a proportional tax τ on labor income. As previously noted, how a government uses its revenues is very important for understanding the impact of labor taxes on labor supply. Let us then consider three different categories of government spending.

The first category is government spending on goods and services that are valued by individuals and that substitute for goods and services individuals would otherwise purchase in the market. Examples of this kind of spending include provision of education and health care services. We denote the per capita spending of this type by G_u, where the subscript u stands for "useful."

The second category is government spending that does not yield anything of value to individuals. Examples of this would include the government hiring unnecessary workers, or hiring workers to produce goods or services that people do not value. We denote the per capita level of this spending by G_w, where the subscript w denotes "wasteful."

The third category of spending is transfer payments, which we denote by T in per capita terms. Examples of transfer payments are programs such as Social Security, disability insurance, and unemployment insurance. The key feature of this type of spending is that the government simply gives money to individuals.

Because we are concerned only with the average effects of taxes and spending, we assume that all individuals are treated equally in terms of both the goods and services that they obtain from the government and the transfer payment that they receive. We assume, too, that the government must balance its budget, so that total spending must equal total revenues.[2] Given recent events, the reader may find the assumption that the government balances its budget to be somewhat at odds with reality. Two comments are in order on this point. First, recall that we are interpreting this model to reflect how much an individual wants to work over his or her lifetime. We similarly interpret the assumption of a balanced budget to mean that government balances its budget over fairly long periods of time. But to the extent that even this assumption may be viewed as empirically not reasonable, I note that the analysis can accommodate the case in which a government runs a deficit over the longer term.

We can now consider how changes in government taxes and spending will influence economy-wide outcomes. I present four results, which are derived formally in the appendix.[3]

Result 1: An increase in taxes used to finance transfers leads to fewer hours of work in the economy.

This result is very intuitive. As emphasized earlier, the main reason for working is to be able to afford consumption. If the government gives money to individuals, with no strings attached, it decreases the incentive for them to work because they no longer need to earn as much income to afford the same amount of consumption. If, for example, the government guarantees everyone over sixty-five a fixed payment, individuals will have less incentive to work, but in the absence of this payment, individuals will have to work enough to accumulate sufficient savings for retirement. This diminished incentive may manifest itself in different ways.

The individual may work fewer hours during prime-age years, or may retire earlier, or may not take a part-time job after retiring from his or her main job.

In fact, we can actually say something stronger than result 1. The reason is that, from the perspective of the recipients, it does not matter if the government gives them a hundred dollars to spend on goods and services, or if the government provides them with a hundred dollars' worth of the goods and services that they were going to purchase.[4]

That leads to the following result.[5]

Result 2: From the perspective of labor supply, there is no difference between transfer payments and useful government spending.

A simple example of this result is that if the government pays for all costs of higher education, then this reduces the incentives for individuals to work, since they no longer need to generate income to pay for college. This lower incentive may manifest itself in many different ways. Parents who were going to help pay the cost of college for their children might choose to work less. They might retire earlier, or one parent might choose not to work. College students who were going to work part time to help cover the costs of college might choose to work less or not at all.

Next we consider the case of taxes used to fund wasteful spending.

Result 3: If all government spending is wasteful, labor taxes have no effect on hours of work.

This result is worth emphasizing, because it would seem to fly in the face of what most individuals assume is a simple and robust piece of economic logic—that higher taxes on labor income will lead individuals to work less. The key to understanding this result is to observe that if all spending is wasteful, then from the individual's perspective, an increase in taxes is the same as a decrease in the level of the real wage w. In either case, the individual gets less consumption per unit of time devoted to work. As argued earlier, while in general a decrease in the wage can lead to either an increase or a decrease in desired hours of work, the empirical evidence tells us that on average, the effect is basically zero. An individual faced with a tax increase and with no change in government services or transfers would again feel two competing forces. On the one hand, the individual would have to work harder to maintain the same standard of living, but on the other hand, the reward for giving up leisure would go down.

Hence, the same empirical observation that tells us that large permanent increases in wages have very little effect on desired hours of work also tells us that changes in the rate at which labor income is taxed will have no effect on desired hours of work if the revenues are used for wasteful spending. For the reader who is suspicious of this result, a simple test is to look at hours of work in rich and poor countries. Although wages are many times higher in rich countries such as the United States, hours of work in poorer countries are typically quite similar.

To pursue this further, consider the case where the government uses revenues to hire unneeded workers. The result—this has no effect on total hours of works—may at first seem surprising. But we can also interpret this case as one in which the official statistics report no effect on total hours of work, even though the true total amount of work being done has decreased. To see this, note that if the government hires unnecessary workers, then although these workers show up on the payroll and are recorded in official employment statistics, it is as if they are not working, since by virtue of being unnecessary, they are not adding to what is produced in the economy. At some level, it is as if the unnecessary workers are receiving a transfer payment from the government, even though they are recorded as employed.

The above results indicate that even if labor taxes are held constant, changes in the allocation of government spending across categories can still lead to changes in hours of work. We state this as our fourth result.

Result 4: If the government keeps tax rates constant but reduces wasteful spending and increases either transfer payments or useful spending, then labor supply will decrease.

We saw above that increases in taxes do not necessarily lead to lower labor supply. The effect depends very much on what the government does with the resulting tax revenues. In one extreme case, in which all of the tax revenue is used to finance wasteful government spending, then there is no effect of taxes on labor supply. However, in the other extreme case, in which all revenues are used either for transfer payments or for useful government spending, then higher taxes necessarily imply lower labor supply. This result expresses what most people would think of as the commonsense consequences of higher taxes on labor supply.[6]

More generally, this result would also obtain as long as some of the increased tax revenue was being used to finance either higher transfer payments or useful government spending. In this sense the statement that higher taxes lead to fewer hours worked is indeed quite a general one. But the magnitude of the effect will very much depend on what fraction of the increased revenues are being used for transfer payments or useful government spending versus wasteful government spending.

The Social Cost of Higher Taxes

There is an important point to note here concerning the issue of whether tax increases should be viewed as a good thing or a bad thing. The previous discussion has focused on whether higher taxes lead to lower hours of work. But we should not jump quickly to the conclusion that just because hours of work are reduced that higher taxes are necessarily bad. Rather, we have to weigh the costs and benefits of the programs that the taxes finance. If the disincentive effects of taxes lead people to work less, then the lost output should be viewed as a cost. But this needs to be weighed against the potential benefits of the programs that the tax revenue will be used to support. The larger the disincentive effects of higher taxes, the greater is the cost of higher taxes, which in turn suggests that only programs with a sufficiently high value can be justified.

It is also important to distinguish between the costs to the economy of two types of taxes, those that fund wasteful government spending and those that fund either useful government spending or transfer payments. In the case of wasteful spending, there is no effect on labor supply, but there is a cost associated with the wasted resources. In the case of useful government spending or transfer payments, there are no wasted resources, but there is still a cost to the economy in the policy's tendency to decrease hours of work. This is a critical point to keep in mind. It is clearly not controversial to argue that wasteful government spending should be eliminated. But even if government spending is providing useful services, there is still a cost associated with it via its depressing effect on labor supply. It follows that the benefits of any program need to be weighed very carefully against these costs.

The Laffer Curve

Given the prominence of the Laffer curve in policy discussions dating back to the Reagan administration, it is interesting to consider how the Laffer curve relates to this discussion of taxes' effects on the labor supply. We begin with a brief summary of the economics that lie behind the Laffer curve.

The Laffer curve represents the relationship between tax rates and tax revenue. Assume for now that the tax revenues are used for purposes such that higher tax rates lead people to work fewer hours, i.e., for either useful government spending or transfer payments. Since tax revenues are the product of the tax rate and income from working, it follows that tax revenues could either increase or decrease when tax rates are increased, depending on how large the decrease in hours worked is. If higher tax rates lead to lower tax revenues, then it would also be true that lower taxes would lead to higher revenues. In such a case it would clearly be beneficial to lower taxes, since this would make individuals happier and would leave the government with even more revenue.

So is the possibility of a downward-sloping Laffer curve just a theoretical possibility, or is it something that could describe the actual situation of some economies? It is surely more than just a theoretical possibility, in the following sense. At a tax rate of 0, it is obvious that the government raises no revenue from the tax. At a tax rate of 100 percent it is also true that the government would raise zero revenue, since there would be no incentive for anyone to do any work. We know from reality that when taxes are in the range of 30 percent, for example, tax revenues are positive. Since they are positive at this point, and they are zero when taxes are as high as 100 percent, it follows that at some point the tax revenues must decrease in the face of further increases in the tax rate.

This implies that the Laffer curve must be downward sloping at some point. The key question is, at what point? In the 1980 presidential election it was suggested that the United States was operating on the downward-sloping portion of the Laffer curve, thus implying that a decrease in taxes would increase both after-tax incomes for individuals and government revenues. Subsequent work has suggested that the United States was in fact still on the upward-sloping portion of the curve.[7]

To summarize, the economics behind the Laffer curve tell us that if we are on the downward-sloping portion of the curve, then it is clearly a good idea to lower taxes. However, it is particularly important for us to note here that the reverse is not true. That is, just because the economy is on the upward-sloping portion of the Laffer curve, it does not follow that it is a bad idea to lower taxes. When the economy is on the upward-sloping portion of the Laffer curve, a decrease in taxes will lead to greater hours of work and more output, but smaller revenues for the government. Some government spending would therefore have to be eliminated (at least in the longer run). It follows that decisions about changes in taxes must weigh the benefits of potentially affected government programs against the cost of the lost output associated with the disincentives for work.

More generally, labor supply responses have implications for the ability of the government to raise additional revenues from higher taxes on labor. Assuming individuals do not change the number of hours they work when the government increases the tax rate by 5 percent, then total revenues will also increase by 5 percent. But if the increase in tax rates leads individuals to work less, then the increase in revenues will be less. So the magnitude of the labor supply response to changes in labor tax rates is very important in predicting how able the government is to increase total revenues by increasing taxes.

Additional Tax Instruments

In the preceding analysis I assumed that the only tax instrument was a tax on labor income levied on workers. This assumption might seem to limit the applicability of the analysis, since in many countries it is payroll taxes levied on firms and value-added (or consumption) taxes that generate the dominant share of government revenues. In this section I show that one can appropriately combine all of these taxes into an effective tax on labor income, so that there is no loss in generality from simply considering a tax on labor income.

In the appendix I derive this result algebraically, but it is important to note that it is very intuitive. The key is to recognize that a tax on labor income distorts the trade-off that an individual faces between leisure and consumption. That is, when the tax on labor income increases, workers obtain less consumption for each unit of leisure that they sacrifice. When the government taxes consumption expenditure instead of labor income, the same effect is present: a given increase in income now buys less consumption, so individuals now face a worse trade-off in terms of the amount of consumption that they can get from a given decrease in leisure.

In the case of a payroll tax the result is the same, though the mechanism is somewhat more subtle. If the government levies a payroll tax on firms, then this increases the cost of labor to firms. This induces firms to hire less labor at the going wage rate, and hence creates excess supply of labor in the labor market. This puts downward pressure on wages, and in order to restore equilibrium the wage must drop by enough to offset the payroll tax. Hence, even though workers do not directly pay the tax, the effect of the tax is to reduce their wages and hence worsen the terms at which they can trade leisure for consumption. The key result is that there is no loss in generality from considering taxes only on labor income. But from a practical perspective, it is critical to keep in mind that consumption and payroll taxes act like a tax on labor income.

Generalizing from the earlier analysis, I now consider three different proportional taxes: a labor income tax levied on workers, denoted by τ_h, a consumption tax levied on consumers, denoted by τ_c, and a payroll tax levied on firms, denoted by τ_p. In the appendix I show that one can define the effective tax on labor, denoted by τ, that properly incorporates all of these different taxes.[8]

Increases in any of τ_h, τ_p, or τ_c lead to an increase in τ. If one uses this value of τ in the earlier analysis, it correctly incorporates the effects of a system that includes all three types of taxes. As a practical matter I note that if the values of all three tax rates are relatively small, say less than 10 percent, then $\tau = \tau_h + \tau_p + \tau_c$ will be a fairly good approximation. But for larger values of these taxes, this approximation is not very accurate; see the appendix for the expression needed to find the equivalent tax.

Additional Spending Policies

In addition to the three categories of spending just mentioned, there are three other spending policies that are worth noting. The first of these concerns spending on public goods such as defense. This spending is not wasteful but also does not substitute for private consumption spending. The second has to do with subsidies to consumption. The third has to do with spending on infrastructure.

We begin with defense spending. The natural way to introduce defense spending into the model is to assume that individuals have preferences given by $u(c,1-h) + f(G_d)$, where G_d denotes spending on defense and f is an increasing function. I will not go through the details, but it turns out that if the government taxes labor income to finance this type of spending, then just as in the case of wasteful spending, there will be no effect on labor supply. However, in contrast to the case of wasteful spending, there is not necessarily a cost to the economy. There is still an important issue concerning the optimal level of spending on defense, so if defense spending is too high, then it does follow that taxes levied to finance defense spending impose a cost. But what is important is that the cost to society in this case is not due to a reduction in the amount of work being done.

Next consider the case in which the tax revenues are used to finance a per-unit subsidy to consumption.[9] Such a subsidy is the same as a negative consumption tax. While subsidies such as this may not be widespread, there are important examples among OECD economies. For example, a notable feature of Scandinavian countries is that they provide very substantial subsidies to child care and elderly care. Intuitively, taxes on labor income worsen the trade-off that an individual faces between leisure and consumption, while a subsidy to consumption improves the trade-off.

Perhaps not surprisingly, if the government uses all of the revenue generated from taxing labor income to offer a subsidy to consumption, the two effects perfectly offset one another, and as a result there will be no effect on hours of work. In this case there will also be no cost to society. The case in which all revenues are used to subsidize consumption is an extreme one. But the more general point is that if some revenue is used to subsidize consumption instead of to fund transfer payments or provide government services free of charge, then the effects on hours worked of a given tax rate will be reduced.

Lastly, we discuss the case of government tax revenues used for infrastructure projects, an especially interesting type of spending to consider, given its emphasis in the recent stimulus package. The idea behind infrastructure projects is that they provide inputs such as transportation and communications that enhance the productivity of individual firms in the economy. From the perspective of effects on labor supply, this turns out to be similar to the case of defense spending. The key is that a permanent increase or decrease in wages leads to effectively no change in hours of work; we know this from empirical evidence. If infrastructure projects do increase productivity, this will lead to higher wages, but as just noted, higher wages by themselves do not lead to greater labor supply. Whether the infrastructure projects are worthwhile requires a cost-benefit analysis that would compare the productivity gains with the cost of the projects.

Summary

This chapter has laid out some basic theory concerning the effect of labor taxes on hours of work. It makes two key points. First, the effect of a labor tax on hours of work is dependent on what the government does with the resulting tax revenues. In the case of wasteful government spending, the effect will be zero, but in the case of transfer payments, the effect is negative. Second, it is important to understand that labor taxes include not only taxes on labor income, but also payroll taxes paid by firms and consumption or value-added taxes.

2

Labor Taxes and Hours of Work: Where to Look for Evidence?

The previous chapter presented the underlying theoretical argument behind the idea that increases in labor taxation impose a cost on the economy by creating disincentives for individuals to work, thereby reducing the output produced by the economy. In particular, it specified the circumstances under which a change in labor taxes is expected to lead to a change in labor supply. A key issue for policymakers is the magnitude of this labor supply effect. If it is very small, then it may be something that policymakers can safely ignore when they weigh the costs and benefits of various tax proposals. But if it is large, then the labor supply effects need to be taken into account in policy analyses of tax changes. So how are we to determine if these effects are small or large? This chapter discusses this question at a somewhat general level and sets the stage for the later and more detailed analysis.

How Do We Know What We Think We Know?

Before proceeding, it is useful to note a few things. The question that concerns us here is but one example of a general issue that economists and policymakers confront on a regular basis: how to determine the magnitude of the effect of a given change in government policy (or some other feature of the economic environment) on individual economic choices and the overall economy. Much research in economics is devoted to this question, and economists disagree about how best to answer it. Attempting to survey the relevant literature is far beyond the scope of this monograph, and would require presentation of a lot of very technical material. Instead, my goal is to broadly describe a couple of approaches found in the literature and mention some general issues associated with the problem of testing economic theories.

It is instructive to first note that the issue of testing and quantifying theories is not specific to economics; it is something that routinely comes up in the physical and biological sciences as well. But while the general issue arises in fields other than economics, the methods that researchers can use vary quite dramatically across fields. For example, the most common approach taken in the physical and biological sciences is to conduct controlled experiments in the laboratory, where the researchers have the ability to keep all elements of the system constant except for the one factor that they want to study. If one wants to know the effect of a particular change when there are no other changes at the same time, running a controlled experiment is an ideal way to obtain the desired information.

Unfortunately, this method is not well suited to learning about the effects of economic policy on the U.S. economy. Reproducing a version of the U.S. economy in the laboratory and then subjecting it to a change in tax rates to observe how it responds is not possible. And getting the U.S. government to run experiments on the actual economy by enacting policies just for the sake of learning about their consequences is not likely to be politically acceptable. Moreover, even if the government was willing to perform such experiments, they would not be controlled experiments, because it would be impossible to hold all other factors constant. This inability to do controlled experiments in the laboratory makes life much more difficult for economists than for other scientists.

One way that economists have responded to this difficulty in the context of the tax question that interests us here is by applying sophisticated statistical techniques to data on individual workers to infer the size of the income and substitution effects. Once we know the magnitudes of these effects, we can calculate how individuals would respond to specific changes in tax and transfer systems. The basic strategy for uncovering the magnitude of the income and substitution effects is the following. If we have data on the choices that an individual worker makes at several points in time, and if the economic conditions that this individual faces change over time, we can use the data on how the individual's economic choices responded to these changes in order to estimate the income and substitution effects. A classic example of this literature is the paper by MaCurdy (1981), which was the first to implement this type of analysis using a dataset that contained information on how the economic choices of a given set of workers changed over time.

The literature that applies this general method is very large. Moreover, much of it concludes that the labor supply effects associated with increased taxation are very small. Loosely speaking, the reason for this is that these studies typically find that workers do not change their hours of work very much in response to changes in labor market conditions.

While the general method followed by this literature is a useful one, and has the potential to produce important information about labor supply responses, many of the existing studies have limitations that severely restrict the scope of the conclusions that can be drawn from them. Although a full appreciation of these issues would require a lot of space and a lot of technical sophistication, some basic points can be appreciated without either. Here I briefly outline three of them.

First, it is important to understand that the results can be very sensitive to the underlying details of the specification that the researcher uses to uncover the size of the income and substitution effects. According to Imai and Keane (2004), for example, researchers will make very different inferences from existing data depending on whether they take into account the fact that younger workers' choices are influenced by the desire to acquire skills and experience so as to obtain higher wages later in life. But there are literally hundreds of papers that have estimated labor supply responses without taking this into account, and these papers form the foundation for what many view as the consensus on small labor supply effects.

Second, once one understands that the labor supply problem for an individual is really about how much to work over a lifetime, i.e., it involves a decision about how much to work when working and also about what fraction of one's life to spend in the labor force, it is apparent that in most cases the existing literature provides only limited information. For example, observing that a forty-year-old married male does not change his hours of work very much when taxes change tells us very little about whether he will change his retirement behavior twenty years in the future, or whether he would choose a different occupation or seek a different level of education if he were starting over again.

Most of the literature that concludes that labor supply effects are small has focused on the changes in hours of work for continuously employed prime-aged male workers and extrapolated that the same must be true for overall hours of work. Recent work by Rogerson and Wallenius (2009) shows that this conclusion is unfounded, and that the small estimates of labor supply responses uncovered in most of this literature have no bearing on the aggregate change in hours in response to a change in taxes used to finance transfer payments.[1]

A third issue has to do with coordination of work schedules. A simple reality of life for most workers is that they are not free to choose how many hours to work at a particular job, since at many establishments hours need to be coordinated across many individuals. Suppose that something changes in the circumstances of one individual worker; to be concrete, consider an assembly-line worker who wants to reduce his hours in order to assist an aging parent. But because he works on an assembly line, where everyone works the same shift length, his hours of work will not change after this change in circumstances. Many economists conclude that because there was no change in work hours for this individual, he did not want to change them. And from this they go on to infer that individuals will not change their labor supply in response to changes in taxes, either.

The message here is that observing how one individual's hours of work change in response to a change in his or her own individual circumstances may not provide much information about what the individual's preferences are. Put somewhat differently, just because everyone at a given firm is working forty hours per week, this does not mean that people want to work forty hours per week, regardless of the circumstances. If there were some change in the overall economy that led to all workers wishing to work fewer hours, then we might expect to see firms changing their shift length. Such changes are consistent with the often dramatic reductions in shift length in the early stages of industrialization.

To summarize this discussion: there is value in the general method of extrapolating from data on individuals' economic choices to conclusions about how the economy as a whole will respond to changes in policy, but much of the work done to date has either produced answers that are very sensitive to assumptions or has drawn broad conclusions that are not warranted. The simple fact is that many economists have misinterpreted the extent to which these results about individuals allow one to extrapolate to provide general answers.

Although the option of conducting explicit controlled experiments is not available, not all hope is lost. It is true that governments would have a hard time enacting a policy change if they were to tell the electorate that it was all just part of an experiment, but the fact is that when one looks back at the U.S. economy over the last fifty years, one sees that policy changes have been enacted repeatedly. Sometimes a policy is enacted with the goal of achieving specific economic effects, or perhaps as the best response to a given situation. Because different politicians and/or different political parties have different views about the effects of specific policies and/or have different objectives, the result is that the U.S. economic record provides us with a lot of "experimental" data. By sifting through these data, the hope is that we can learn something about the effects of specific policies on the U.S. economy.

This too turns out to be very difficult, and interpreting the available data is by no means a straightforward process. But it can be done so long as we are aware of certain pitfalls. In the remainder of this chapter I suggest how to avoid these pitfalls as they apply to our question of interest, the effect of tax changes on labor supply.

Experimental Data from the Economy

The first point to understand is that at any point in time there are many changes taking place in the U.S. economy (or any other economy, for that matter), and that these changes might have implications for aggregate hours of work. As a result, although a change in tax rates might occur in some particular year, it is likely that there are some other changes taking place at the same time, many of which might also be affecting the labor market and hence hours of work. When the laboratory is the economy of a large country, it is impossible to hold all factors constant except one.

A recent example from the United States might be instructive here. In 2008 the government issued stimulus checks to many households in the economy. A key question of interest to policymakers concerned the effect this would have on consumer spending. But just as the stimulus package was passed and the checks were mailed out, the price of oil (and therefore gasoline) skyrocketed, and news began to spread of impending problems in both the credit and housing markets. These circumstances make it very difficult to disentangle the effect of the stimulus checks on consumer spending from the effect of all of the other factors. If the desired effect of the stimulus checks was to increase consumer spending relative to what would have happened in the absence of the stimulus checks, then the key question is what would have happened to consumer spending if the stimulus checks had not been mailed out. But this is not something that can easily be deduced from just looking at actual economic data, since the data necessarily include the effects of all of the other changes that were taking place in the economy at the same time.

In short, the aggregate time series data do not present us with a controlled experiment, since it is generally not the case that only one thing is changing in the economy at any particular point in time. One of the most common mistakes that can be made in interpreting economic data for a period in which many different changes in the economic environment occurred is to attribute all of the resulting changes in economic outcomes to just one of these changes.

Consider recent policy discussions about taxes and labor supply. As we will see in the next chapter, the decade of the 1990s was a period of strong growth in the U.S. economy. In addition to robust growth in output, investment, and productivity, this decade witnessed a sharp increase in hours of work. There was also an increase in labor taxes during this period. Some commentators have concluded that, because this period witnessed an increase in hours worked at the same time that taxes on labor were increased, taxes on labor do not depress labor supply. But the fallacy of this argument is clear: unless one can control for the underlying cause of the dramatic expansion in overall economic activity, one cannot conclude anything from this episode about the effect of labor taxes on labor supply, holding all else constant.[2] The data represent the net effect of many simultaneous changes, and so we are faced with the difficult problem of trying to disentangle the effects of the various changes that were taking place.

But to state the problem with looking at the aggregate time series data is also to suggest circumstances in which it might be less severe. The economy can never produce a controlled experiment. But a situation where one of the variables changes much more than any of the other variables has the potential to mimic a controlled experiment. In the context of labor taxes and hours of work, the U.S. data do not provide us with a true controlled experiment, since there have been many changes throughout the last fifty years that might affect hours of work. However, if the change in the tax rate on labor were sufficiently large, then it is more likely that the change in the tax rate is the dominant change. And in this case we might reasonably think that we are observing something closer to a controlled experiment. Conversely, the smaller the change in tax rates, the more likely it is that other changes are of similar or greater importance than the tax change, which means that we do not have something that approaches a controlled experiment.

To be sure, this approach may not provide definitive evidence, since there is the danger that we might be neglecting some other change that turns out to be very important. But I would argue that this type of evidence, if available, seems a very useful starting point for estimates of the likely magnitude of labor supply responses to changes in labor taxes. One advantage of this approach is its relative transparency.

An important issue, then, is whether the U.S. economy has actually provided us with such a situation. It might seem that even one episode in the U.S. data in which we see a large change in labor taxes would make it possible to infer the effect of labor taxes on labor supply. It turns out that this is not enough. Specifically, there are two other considerations that are important. The first is that the tax changes should be permanent and not temporary. The second is that sufficient time should have elapsed to allow individuals to fully respond to the changes in taxes.

I begin with the temporary-versus-permanent distinction. In general, the effects of changes in some specific policy might differ depending upon whether the policy is adopted temporarily or permanently. (Of course, one may argue that policy changes are never truly permanent, so the key distinction here is whether a given change is likely to be reversed in the near future.) Economic theory and common sense both dictate that people will respond differently to changes in tax policy depending upon whether they think the changes are temporary or permanent.[3] If the labor supply response to temporary changes in taxes does not necessarily provide useful information about the labor supply response to permanent changes in taxes, it follows that episodes such as the Clinton tax increases or the Bush tax cuts are not likely to yield the information that we are interested in.

Next, consider the issue of allowing for sufficient time to elapse. It is important to understand that the changes in labor supply induced by permanent changes in tax rates may take place gradually. Many individuals are implicitly or explicitly committed in the short run in terms of consumption expenditures (e.g., mortgage payments or car payments), and may take time to implement any changes in labor supply that will bring about changes in consumption, including such things as moving to a more or less expensive house or apartment, or buying a more or less expensive car.

Moreover, somebody who has already accumulated a lot of work experience is in a very different situation from someone who is just entering the labor force, so we may not observe all the longer-term effects of tax changes until we see the outcomes for the newest workers. As noted in the last chapter, there is also a dynamic aspect to labor supply: if an individual responds to changes in taxes by postponing his or her planned date of retirement, the labor supply adjustment may not show up until later. And if it takes some time for individuals to perceive that a change is indeed permanent, they will not immediately make the appropriate changes to their behavior.[4]

Summary

To draw conclusions about the effect of tax changes on labor supply, we would ideally like to observe changes in tax rates that are both large and permanent and that occurred sufficiently long ago for individuals to have adjusted their economic behavior in response. This type of direct evidence is available—but as the next chapter makes clear, only in the experiences of countries other than the United States.

3

Taxes, Government Spending, and Hours of Work in the United States

It is natural for a policymaker who is interested in the effect of tax changes on the U.S. economy to first look for evidence from the U.S. experience. This chapter carries out the first step in such an analysis. In particular, it documents the facts regarding changes in labor taxes, government spending, and hours of work for the U.S. economy in the period subsequent to 1956. The year 1956 is chosen as the starting point for the analysis due to issues of data availability. But given the importance of both World War II and the Great Depression in the period from 1930 to the mid-1940s, restricting attention to this period is probably a good idea in any case. After laying out the facts in this chapter, I ask what conclusions we can draw from these facts.

U.S. Tax Rates on Labor

We begin by looking at the evolution of tax rates on labor in the United States. It is important to note several issues that combine to make measuring the economy-wide tax rate on labor a complicated task.

One issue is that different individuals face different tax rates, so that even if we knew the tax rate faced by each individual, we would still have to appropriately average these rates. The second issue is that it is not so easy to infer the labor tax rate faced by a given individual. In part, this is because individuals do not actually face tax rates; rather, they face tax schedules, which is to say that their tax rate depends upon their taxable income. The U.S. tax code features a progressive tax on income, with marginal tax rates increasing with income and the current maximum rate set at 35 percent. Social Security contributions, on the other hand, are a constant fraction of labor earnings up to a maximum (currently equal to $102,000), after which they drop to zero. To make matters more difficult, when married individuals file jointly, the income tax rate that a given individual faces on additional labor income depends not only on this individual's income but also on the spouse's income.

But most important, even knowing the tax schedule and the income of all individuals in a household does not make it possible to infer the actual tax rate that would apply to this household if it experienced an increase in labor income. The reason for this is that the tax code allows for a host of deductions, and so an individual's true tax rate is potentially quite different from the tax rate that one might infer simply by looking at tax schedules. For example, the deductibility of home mortgage interest payments can lead to a large reduction in tax liability if an individual itemizes deductions. Some income is not taxable if allocated to particular categories of spending. Important examples are charitable contributions, worker contributions for firm-provided health insurance, retirement accounts, and flexible spending accounts. (Of course, if retirement contributions are not taxed currently, they will be taxed in the future when income is drawn from the retirement account.)

That said, there are several studies that have produced measures of tax rates on labor and how they have changed over time. The tax rates that I will base my analysis on were computed by McDaniel (2006), who used Prescott's (2004) modification of the procedure originally used by Mendoza, Razin, and Tesar (1994). Of particular importance is that this procedure can be used to infer labor tax rates for several OECD countries dating back to 1960. Here I will briefly describe the procedure, though I refer the reader to the sources noted above for more detail.

The basic strategy is to take all tax revenues collected by governments (at all three levels—local, state, and federal) and allocate them according to which source they are derived from: labor income, capital income, consumption expenditures, or investment expenditures. For most tax revenue this can be done without problems. For example, payroll taxes are a tax derived from labor income.

Some tax revenues cannot be uniquely allocated to a particular underlying source, and so in these cases the revenue must be allocated across categories. For example, proprietor's income reflects a return to both capital and labor, and so taxes on proprietor's income must be allocated between taxes on capital income and taxes on labor income. The assumption is that the capital and labor income share in proprietor's income is the same as it is in the rest of the economy. Similarly, tax revenue from income taxation is a mix of capital and labor taxation, since these sources of income are combined to infer taxable income.

Having allocated tax revenues to all of the categories, one then computes the appropriate base for each revenue source, which similarly requires some assumptions in order to separate income into capital and labor components. The average effective tax rate for each source is then computed as the ratio of tax revenue from each source divided by the corresponding tax base. These are the measures that I will use in what follows. As in chapter 1, the tax rates on labor income and consumption are combined to yield an average effective tax on labor.

One important limitation of this procedure is that it does not attempt to control for the difference between marginal tax rates and average tax rates. To the extent that this difference is relatively constant over time, this will not matter much for an analysis that focuses on changes in tax rates over time. But if there are periods in which we see large changes in the relationship between marginal and average tax rates, this would need to be taken into account.

Figure 3-1 shows the time series for the average effective tax rate on labor. There are two curves in the figure. The dashed line is the actual tax rate computed using the procedure described above. As is commonly observed with these types of tax measures, the tax rate tends to decline during recessions and increase during expansions. It is important to keep in mind that these tax rates are not statutory tax rates, and so movements here do not necessarily reflect changes in statutory rates. For example, holding the tax schedule fixed and considering the progressivity in the federal income tax schedule, we would expect to see average labor taxes increase when income is relatively high and decrease when average income is relatively low. Because of such movements, plus the possibility of year-to-year variation induced by measurement error, it is probably best to focus on the solid line, which shows the trend behavior of the average effective tax on labor.

The solid line shows a relatively steady upward trend, with an overall increase of about eight or nine percentage points. The bulk of the increase occurs in the first part of the period, say 1960–1975, with relatively little increase occurring later in the period. One can see a decrease in tax rates at

FIGURE 3-1

AVERAGE U.S. EFFECTIVE RATE TAX ON LABOR INCOME, 1956–2003

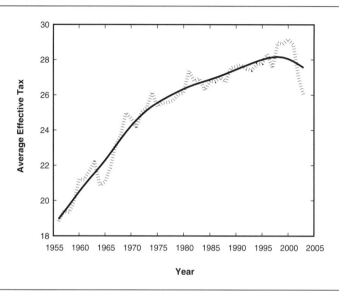

SOURCE: McDaniel 2006.

the end of the sample, and the trend line picks up part of this decrease. It is important to keep in mind that this tax series reflects taxes on labor income at the federal, state, and local level in addition to payroll taxes and taxes on consumption, whereas it is common in many discussions of tax policy to focus solely on the federal tax rates on labor income.

I mentioned above the concern regarding the potential difference between changes in average tax rates and changes in marginal tax rates. Several authors have computed time series measures for marginal tax rates averaged across the population. One of these is Joines (1981). His series has been extended by McGrattan, Rogerson, and Wright (1997). In figure 3-2 I plot the series from figure 3-1 and the series from McGrattan, Rogerson, and Wright for the period of overlap.

Both series show the gradual and steady increase from the beginning of the period through the mid-1970s. At that point the two series exhibit somewhat different behavior. The series for marginal tax rates shows a fairly large increase in the late 1970s, followed by a sharp decline in the

FIGURE 3-2

AVERAGE AND MARGINAL U.S. TAX RATES ON LABOR, 1956–1992

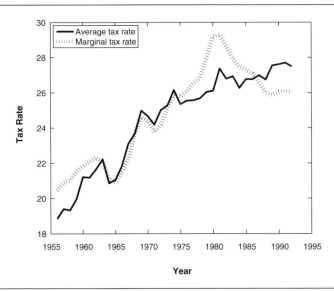

SOURCES: McDaniel 2006 (for average tax rate); McGrattan, Rogerson, and Wright 1997 (for marginal tax rate).

early 1980s, and by 1992 it is roughly back at its 1975 level. On the other hand, the average tax rate is relatively flat from 1980 on. Over the entire period, the series for average tax rates shows an increase of about eight points, while the series for marginal tax rates shows an increase of about six points. So, while the two series behave somewhat differently over the 1975–1990 period, in terms of the overall change, the two are similar.

It is perhaps of interest to note that some simple measures of the size of government show similar trends, both qualitatively and quantitatively. This is consistent with the fact that most government revenues are derived from taxes on labor. Figure 3-3 plots the trend for current receipts of government relative to GDP for the United States. Like the tax rate picture, this curve shows a steady increase through to the late seventies. Unlike the previous figure, it shows a slight decrease associated with the Reagan years, but then slowly increases through the 1990s. Overall the increase is around five percentage points.

FIGURE 3-3

CURRENT RECEIPTS OF GOVERNMENT AS PERCENTAGE OF GDP, 1960–2000

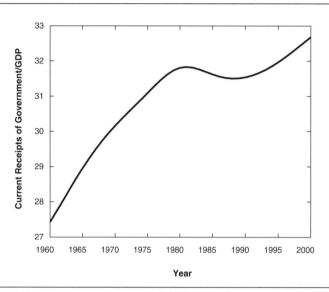

SOURCE: *OECD Historical Statistics* (Paris: OECD Publishing) for the years specified.

Another way to measure the size of government is to look at total spending of government. Figure 3-4 shows the total outlays of government relative to GDP. This curve also exhibits a steady rise through the late 1970s, and the overall increase is about six percentage points. A slight difference from the previous curves is that spending as a share of GDP continues to increase through the mid-1980s, but then decreases steadily through the 1990s. The difference between the figures for current receipts of government and total outlays of government is accounted for by the fact that the Reagan years saw a sharp increase in the deficit.

To summarize, labor taxes in the United States since 1956 seem to show a gradual but steady increase, with the greatest increase occurring prior to 1980. Overall, the increase over the entire period is about eight or nine percentage points if based on changes in average tax rates, somewhat less if based on the change in marginal tax rates.

At this point it is interesting to ask whether the changes in labor taxes for the United States satisfy the three criteria (permanent, not recent,

FIGURE 3-4

TOTAL OUTLAYS OF GOVERNMENT AS PERCENTAGE OF GDP, 1960–2000

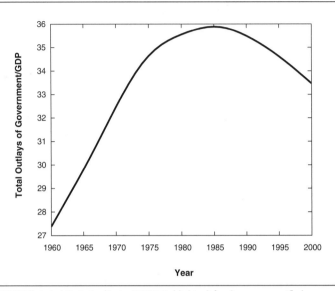

SOURCE: *OECD Historical Statistics* (Paris: OECD Publishing) for the years specified.

and large) that we set out in the last chapter. First, the increase in taxes certainly seems permanent. The different measures considered tell somewhat different stories about whether the period from 1975 to 1990 witnessed either relatively flat tax rates or an increase followed by a decrease, but in either case it is clear that taxes after 2000 are higher than taxes in 1956. While tax rates have decreased slightly since 2000, this does not change the fact that overall there has been a significant long-term increase.

The second criterion was that sufficient time should have passed to allow individuals to fully respond to the changes in taxes. Given that most of the overall increase occurred by the mid-1970s, it seems safe to assume that this is the case.

The third criterion was that the change in taxes should be large, or rather large relative to other possible changes that would also affect the labor market. This is somewhat more difficult to judge. The size of the overall increase is on the order of eight percentage points, perhaps a little bit less, depending upon the measure used. This is sizable, but it needs to be compared to other changes that have also occurred over this same period. In fact, I will argue later that this tax change is not large relative to other changes, and that the larger changes are likely to obscure the effects of taxes. But before I make that case, I document some properties of government spending.

Properties of Government Spending in the United States

In view of the theory discussed in chapter 1, it is relevant to ask what the increased tax revenues have been used for. After all, one message of chapter 1 was that if the additional tax revenues were all being used to finance wasteful government spending, then we should not expect to see an impact on hours of work. As a practical matter it is not possible to trace how tax revenues from a particular source are ultimately spent, so we will have to be content to simply look at overall patterns in government spending.

Chapter 1 emphasized that wasteful government spending on goods and services is distinct from either transfer payments or useful government spending on goods and services. While there is plenty of anecdotal evidence describing examples of wasteful government spending, there are no time series measures available to tell us how large this category is and how it has changed over time. But for our purposes this is probably not particularly important. To see why, we begin with a look at the behavior of government transfer payments over time. Figure 3-5 shows the ratio of transfer payments to GDP for the United States.

This figure shows the same basic properties as the figure for average labor tax rates (figure 3-1). That is, there is an increase of about seven percentage points over the entire period, with the bulk of the increase coming prior to 1980. Not surprisingly, this ratio fluctuates over the business cycle, with transfer payments relative to GDP increasing during recessions and decreasing during expansions. This reflects the basic fact that during recessions there are more individuals who receive some form of income support from various programs, including, for example, the unemployment insurance program. The key point to take away from figure 3-5 is that the increase in labor tax rates in the United States over the last fifty years has been associated with a roughly comparable increase in the scale of government transfer programs.

FIGURE 3-5

GOVERNMENT TRANSFERS AS A PERCENTAGE OF GDP, 1960–2005

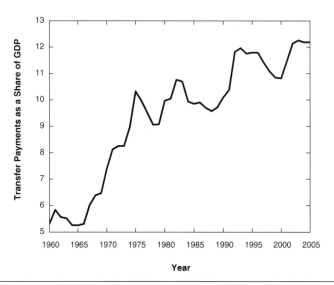

SOURCE: *Economic Report of the President* for the years specified, available at http://www.gpoaccess.gov/eop/.

Another component of spending that is of interest is expenditures on national defense. I argued in chapter 1 that if increased tax revenues are used to finance these expenditures, then it is not likely to lead to changes in aggregate hours worked. Similarly, if taxes are held constant and expenditure is shifted from defense spending to what I labeled "useful" spending, then we would expect to see a negative impact on hours of work. Figure 3-6 shows the ratio of federal spending on national defense relative to GDP for the United States. We can see that there has been a marked decline in the share of GDP going to spending on national defense.

Figure 3-7 shows the ratio of government spending on goods and services (also called government consumption) to GDP. Note that the level of government spending on goods and services relative to GDP is basically the same in 2005 as it was in 1960, so that over the entire period there has been little change in this value. Combining this with the earlier figure for spending on defense (figure 3-6), we see that the reduction in spending on national defense reflects a reallocation of government spending from national defense

FIGURE 3-6

DEFENSE SPENDING AS A PERCENTAGE OF GDP, 1960–2005

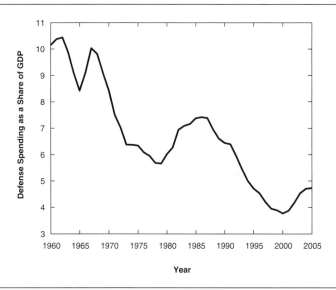

SOURCE: *Economic Report of the President* for the years specified; available at http://www.gpoaccess.gov/eop/.

into other areas. While there has been effectively no change in government spending on goods and services relative to GDP between 1960 and 2005, there have been some interesting changes during the intervening years.

Finally, it is also of interest to look at the behavior of nondefense spending on goods and services relative to GDP. This is shown in figure 3-8. This category shows a marked increase between 1960 and 2005, but virtually all of the increase occurs in the 1960s. After 1970 until around 1985, this ratio decreases slightly; it then begins a gradual increase. As of 2005 this ratio is roughly at its 1970 level, which is about five percentage points higher than in 1960.

The basic story that emerges is this: First, there has been a marked increase in spending on transfer programs. Second, there has also been a marked decrease in spending on national defense. Third, the decrease in spending on national defense has effectively resulted in a reallocation of government spending away from defense and toward other goods and services.

If we interpret these changes from the perspective of the theory laid out in chapter 1 and the increase in tax rates documented in the previous

FIGURE 3-7

GOVERNMENT CONSUMPTION AS A PERCENTAGE OF GDP, 1960–2005

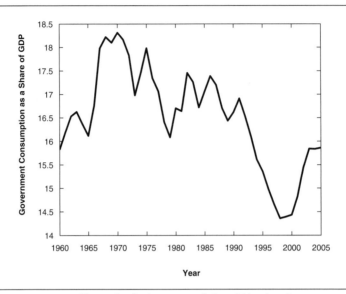

SOURCE: *Economic Report of the President* for the years specified; available at http://www.gpoaccess.gov/eop/.

section, then we infer the following. The large increase in transfers that accompanied the increase in labor tax rates leads us to expect that aggregate hours of work should decrease. The extent of the decrease would depend on the strength of the disincentive effect. The reallocation of spending away from national defense and toward other categories also leads us to expect a decrease in hours, as long as none of the increased spending on goods and services was wasteful. It follows that the changes in spending that have accompanied the changes in labor tax rates are such that we would expect to see decreases in hours of work if the disincentive effects discussed in chapter 2 are indeed significant.

Hours of Work in the United States

The data that I use for hours of work come from two sources: the Organis-ation for Economic Cooperation and Development and the Groningen Growth and

FIGURE 3-8
NONDEFENSE SPENDING AS A PERCENTAGE OF GDP, 1960–2005

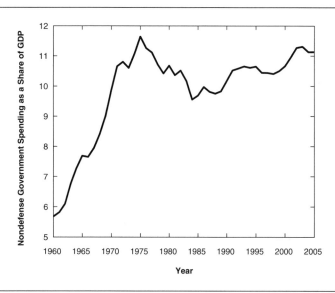

SOURCE: *Economic Report of the President* for the years specified; available at http://www.gpoaccess.gov/eop/.

Development Center (GGDC). These data sets provide access to comparable data on hours of work for several countries, which is important for my purposes since in a later chapter I will be comparing experiences across countries.

To compute total hours of work for the economy, I take the product of two numbers: the number of civilian individuals employed and the measure of annual hours worked per employed person. This latter measure attempts to take into account not only the length of the standard workweek, but also the number of vacation days that a worker has, the number of statutory holidays, and time lost due to things such as sickness or strikes. I want to emphasize the importance of taking all of these factors into account, especially in connection with the cross-country comparisons. It is common for economists and policymakers to use data that are based on payrolls of private establishments. Because workers get paid when they are using vacation days, and in many cases for statutory holidays as well, these payroll data reflect hours of work paid for, but not necessarily hours of actual work. It turns out that across countries, the difference in the number of vacation days and the number of statutory holidays is quite large, so this is an important factor to take into account.

If multiplying the number of workers by hours per worker provides us with a measure of total hours of work being carried out in the economy, and if the population of the United States is growing over time, then to determine how much work is being done on average at the level of the individual, we need to divide this value by some measure of the population. We could choose different measures depending on what we believe is the relevant population available for work—for example, all individuals, or all individuals who are fifteen or older, or all individuals who are between fifteen and seventy-five.

For the analysis that I carry out, the precise group does not matter very much, and so in part to ensure that comparable data are available across countries, I choose to use the population aged fifteen to sixty-four as my reference group. This is what is commonly referred to as the size of the working-age population. I make one final adjustment, which is to divide this measure of total annual hours per person of working age by 52 so that it represents weekly hours rather than annual hours. The simple reason for this is that it is easier for most people to think in terms of hours per week rather than hours per year.

It is important to emphasize that this measure is not the same as the average weekly hours per worker. The measure I am looking at takes into account the fact that many people do not work, and this is reflected in the average. If, for example, two-thirds of the population worked forty hours per work and one-third of the population did not work at all, my measure would imply that average weekly hours per person are 26.7. It is absolutely essential that the nonworkers be included in this calculation, since one of the big potential effects of transfer programs such as disability insurance, Social Security, and unemployment insurance is to influence the number of people who are not working.

Figure 3-9 displays the behavior of weekly hours per person of working age for the United States over the period 1956–2006. Once again, two lines are drawn on the figure, with the dashed line being the actual data and the solid line being a smoothed version of the actual data, in order to help us better see the trends. As is well known, hours worked fluctuate up and down as the economy passes through the expansions and recessions associated with the business cycle. The dashed line indicates these cyclical

FIGURE 3-9

WEEKLY HOURS WORKED IN THE U.S., 1956–2006

(per person aged 15–64)

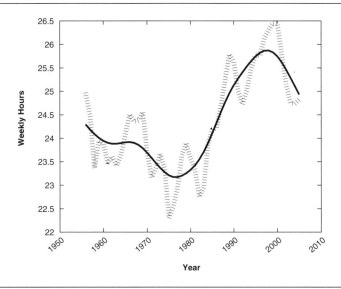

SOURCES: Hours from GGDC (http://www.conference-board.org/economics/database.cfm); population from OECD (http://stats.oecd.org/index.aspx?r=861732).

movements, with large decreases evident in the large recessions that occurred in 1974–1975 and 1982.

There are some important movements of the solid line that are worth noting. First, hours worked tend to drift down gradually over the period 1956–1980. The extent of the decrease is about 4 percent. Second, there is a rather substantial increase in hours worked during the 1980s and 1990s, with hours worked peaking during 2001. Since 2001 there has been a downward trend in hours worked, and as of 2006, hours worked (according to the solid line) are roughly the same as in 1990. Because the solid line takes out the fluctuations associated with business cycles, it should be noted that the comparison between 2006 and 1990 is not being influenced by cyclical considerations.

This last observation is interesting in its own right. During the 1990s the U.S. economy was booming, with high rates of investment, high growth in output, high hours of work, and high productivity growth. As the good times persisted, it was not clear if this was a temporary phenomenon or one that would last for a very long time. There was an active debate among policymakers about whether this represented a "New Economy." It now seems clear, at least from the perspective of the labor market, that the 1990s represented a passing phenomenon. Nonetheless, although hours worked in 2006 are roughly the same as in 1990, they are still significantly higher than they were in 1980, and there is no indication that this increase will not persist.

Of primary importance is the overall change in hours of work during the entire period. Looking at figure 3-9 we see that hours worked in 2006 are somewhat higher than they were fifty years earlier. The extent of the increase is on the order of about 5 percent.

Summary

This chapter has described the changes in labor taxes, government spending, and hours of work in the United States over the last fifty years. In the next chapter we will ask what can be learned from these data about the size of the disincentive effects of labor taxes on hours of work.

4

What We Learn from the U.S. Experience

Having described in some detail what happened with labor taxes, government spending, and hours worked in the United States over the last fifty years, I now put all these data together to see what we learn about the effects of labor tax increases on hours worked. If we look at the overall change from the mid-1950s to the present, we see that both labor tax rates and hours of work have increased. We might be tempted to conclude that there is no evidence in the aggregate U.S. time series data that increases in labor taxes have a significant negative effect on aggregate hours of work; we might even conclude that tax increases have a positive effect on hours of work.

I will discuss later in this chapter why such a conclusion is not warranted. Here, I suggest that a more detailed look at the data also proves interesting. I previously documented that the large increase in taxes occurred prior to 1980 (recall figures 3-1, 3-2). Looking at the figure for hours worked (figure 3-9), we see that there is a significant decrease in hours worked in the United States over the period 1956 to 1980. During this period, taxes increase by about five percentage points and hours worked decrease by about four percentage points. It is the period after 1980 that overturns this relationship. In the period after 1980 there is a small increase in the tax rate on labor, and a very substantial increase in hours of work.

Looking at these two subperiods we might conclude that there is no consistent evidence of a significant negative effect of labor tax rates on hours of work. This is different from saying there is *no* evidence of a significant negative effect of labor tax rates on hours of work. But from the perspective of a policymaker who wants to know if this effect is something that needs to be taken into account in evaluating different policy options, this is certainly not very satisfactory.

In the remainder of this chapter I will show why it is wrong to conclude that the U.S. experience offers no evidence of labor taxes decreasing labor supply. Instead, I will argue that making inferences based on the U.S. experience is problematic because the U.S. experience does not meet one of the three key criteria that allow meaningful inferences: as I will show, the change in labor taxes in the United States is not the dominant change affecting labor supply during the relevant time period. I will argue that once we take this into account, the evidence suggests a very significant negative impact of labor taxes on labor supply.

The Missing Factor

If changes in labor taxes were not the dominant influence on the U.S. economy, then what was responsible for the large changes in labor supply over the last fifty years? It was the very well-documented trend of increasing participation of women in the labor market. To provide one look at this trend, figure 4-1 shows the employment-to-population ratio for women in the age group fifteen through sixty-four. To contrast the differing behavior of men and women over this time period I have also included the same ratio for men. We can see that since 1956 the employment-to-population ratio for women increased from just below 0.4 to almost 0.7. During the same time period, the employment-to-population ratio for men dropped from around 0.9 to around 0.8.

There is a sizable literature in economics that attempts to pinpoint the underlying factors behind the increased participation of women. Various candidates have been proposed, including changing social norms, changes in the cost and availability of child care, changes in contraception, changes in the physical demands of work associated with the rise of the service sector, and changes in the returns to experience.[1]

For our purposes it is not critical to ascertain the relative importance of these different explanations. What is critical is to understand that something big has been going on in the labor market quite apart from the increase in labor tax rates. To be sure, labor taxes might influence the extent to which this big underlying force leads women to work in the market. But unless we take this force into account, we are likely to make mistaken inferences about the effect of taxes.

FIGURE 4-1

EMPLOYMENT-TO-POPULATION RATIOS FOR MALES AND FEMALES, 1956–2000

(per person aged 15–64)

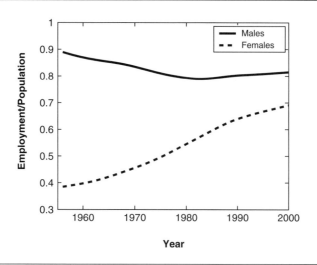

Year

SOURCE: OECD (http://stats.oecd.org/index.aspx?r=861732).

It is interesting to note the contrasting behavior of men and women in figure 4-1. The force behind women's increased participation in the labor market is so pronounced—is presumably so much more important than changes in taxes—that one might think that the effect of taxes cannot properly be inferred from changes in the labor supply of women. One might think instead that the labor supply of males, rather than overall labor supply, would allow inferences about the effect of taxes.

Using this approach and simply looking at the employment rate of males, one sees roughly a 10 percent drop overall between 1956 and 2000, with the bulk of the drop occurring by around 1980. This lines up quite well with the changes in tax rates that we have documented earlier. However, there is good reason to be suspicious of this approach, absent additional information: it could be that men are working less *as a result of* women working more, and so we would be misinterpreting the decline in male labor supply by attributing it to taxes when it is really due to something else. In what follows I will describe a better way to try to take account of the increase in women's labor force participation. I begin by extending our basic model of labor supply.

Home Production and Labor Supply

Thus far, my analysis has been based on the model of labor supply that serves as the benchmark model presented in any undergraduate textbook on labor economics. This model stresses the key trade-off between leisure and consumption that is central to understanding an individual's choice of how much to work.

This model of labor supply implicitly assumes that individuals have two uses for their time: either they can use it to work and earn income, or they can use it for leisure. This becomes problematic when we try to interpret some things that we see in the real world, in particular the dramatic increase in female labor force participation. If leisure and market work are the only two uses of time, then this model says that prior to the dramatic rise in female labor force participation, women were necessarily enjoying a lot of leisure time. In fact, this is clearly not the case, since the traditional housewife devoted considerable time to many household activities that were most definitely work. In order to incorporate this reality into our model, this section considers a third use of time, which—following Becker (1965)—economists have termed home production.[2]

This concept is meant to capture the fact that not all time away from one's job is necessarily used in leisure. Most individuals devote a considerable amount of time to various activities that they could pay someone else to do but instead choose to do themselves. Typical examples include household chores (cleaning, laundry, yard work), meal preparation, and child or elderly care.

To incorporate this concept into our analysis, we now distinguish between time devoted to working in the market, denoted by h_m, and time devoted to home production, denoted by h_n. Leisure time is what is left over, so that if we again normalize the total amount of time available as 1, then leisure is simply $1 - h_m - h_n$. We also need to model the fact that time spent in home production produces something of value to the individual (or household). Consistent with our earlier specification, we now write the utility function as $u[g(c,h_n),1 - h_m - h_n]$, where the function $g(c,h_n)$ can be thought of as representing total consumption, and depends on both how much consumption the individual purchases in the market (c) and how much time is devoted to home production.

A commonly used specification for the function g is the constant elasticity of substitution function, with a key parameter being the extent to which goods and time can be substituted for each other in terms of producing utility.[3] Of course, each different activity may have better or worse market substitutes. For example, by substituting time for market goods, one may be able to prepare a meal at home that is equivalent to what one might purchase in a restaurant. And one might easily choose to paint one's house as a way to substitute time for market goods. But it may not be easy to substitute one's own time for an expensive medical procedure. So this specification needs to be understood as representing the average degree of substitutability within the relevant range of activities.[4]

A key feature of this extended model is that changes in hours of market work do not necessarily represent offsetting changes in leisure. For example, suppose that there is a change in preferences that involves an increased preference for market-produced goods relative to home-produced goods. Examples could include having an increased preference for eating out as opposed to eating at home, or becoming more comfortable with the idea of using market-provided day care services. The main impact of such a change is to lead the individual to change the allocation of his or her working time between market work and home production in the direction of spending a greater fraction of working time engaged in market work. That is, if someone becomes more comfortable using market-provided day care services, then we would expect that he or she is more likely to increase the time devoted to market work and to decrease the time spent in home production. The change in leisure time will be much smaller than the change in time devoted to market work.

This extended model also takes account of a change in the productivity of time devoted to market work relative to that of time devoted to home production. This type of change induces the same types of effects as an increase in the preference for market goods. That is, the dominant effect is to create a reallocation of working time from home production to market production, with a much smaller change in leisure time.

How does this extended framework influence the analysis of tax policies carried out earlier? The earlier model had one decision for an individual: how to allocate available time between work and leisure. The current model now has two decisions: how to allocate available time between work and leisure, and how to allocate working time between market work and home production. While the algebraic analysis is now somewhat more complicated because the number of decisions made by an individual has increased, it is easy to describe the main results.

I emphasize that our previous analysis continues to be relevant for understanding the allocation of time between leisure and work. Specifically, a tax and transfer scheme will lead individuals to work less and enjoy more leisure. And the implications for the allocation of working time are intuitive: taxes on labor income lead individuals to substitute out of market work and into home production, because home production activities are not taxed.

However, it is important to note that this effect is present even if the tax is being used to finance wasteful government spending. While it is no longer the case that taxes used to finance wasteful spending do not influence hours of market work, it remains true that the effect on hours of market work is much larger if the taxes are used to finance a transfer payment (or useful government spending) than if they are used to finance wasteful spending.

Now, suppose that two changes occur at the same time: there is both an increase in an individual's desire to consume market goods relative to home goods (or an increase in market wages relative to the productivity of time spent in home production) and an increase in τ, the tax on labor. The first increase is intended as one way to capture the underlying force behind the increased involvement of women in market production. As just noted, this increase is predicted to lead to an increase in hours of market work, while the increase in τ is predicted to lead to a decrease in hours of market work. Even if the effect of the increase in τ on market work is negative, we might still observe an increase in market work if the first change is sufficiently large.

But this analysis also suggests a method for uncovering the pure effect of the increase in τ on hours of market work. To see this, note that the change in desire for market goods relative to home goods leads primarily to a reallocation of working time between home and market work, with relatively little effect on leisure. In contrast, the effect of the tax is to increase both leisure time and time spent in home production. One way to gauge the effect of the change in preferences for market goods on the amount of market work is to look at the reduction in time spent on home production. Specifically, if this change causes time to be reallocated from home production to market work, then the size of the decrease in home production tells us about the magnitude of the effect on market work.

It follows that if we had data on the change in time devoted to home production, we could try to isolate the effect of taxes on market work by removing the effect of the increase in preferences for market goods (or the increase in market wages relative to time spent in home production). It turns out that such data are available, and in the next section we pursue this strategy.

Changes in Home and Market Work

Whereas data on hours of market work are gathered by official statistical agencies of the government and are readily available, there are no comparable data available for time devoted to home production going back in time. In 2003 the Bureau of Labor Statistics initiated the American Time Use Survey (ATUS), which gathers information about time devoted to home production that is comparable to the data gathered about time devoted to market work. There are also smaller surveys that were conducted at a few points in time prior to 2003. In particular, there are surveys available for the years 1965, 1975, 1985, and 1993. Recent papers by Aguiar and Hurst (2007a) and Francis and Ramey (2009) have analyzed these data to present a picture of how market work, home-production time, and leisure have changed over time. In what follows I will make use of several of the findings in Aguiar and Hurst.

There are a few measurement issues that merit some discussion before we look at the actual data. In particular, exactly which activities are included in home-production time? For the surveys prior to the beginning of the ATUS, data are collected through time diaries. That is, individuals in the sample were asked to record how they spent each fifteen-minute interval of their time over the course of the day. These surveys were administered on different days of the week and at different times of the year, and so can then be aggregated accordingly to reflect overall time use. There were many different categories of time use that individuals could choose from to indicate how they spent a given fifteen-minute interval. Examples included market work, commuting to work, household chores (such as laundry, cooking, cleaning, or yard work), home repair, shopping, attending school, watching TV, exercising, sleeping, child care, personal care, etc.

The issue is how to divide the various categories into the three time uses that we have emphasized in our model of home production: market work, home production, and leisure. As is standard, Aguiar and Hurst remove time devoted to sleep and personal care, treating these as time commitments that are essentially nondiscretionary. In standard surveys, time devoted to market work includes only time actually spent at work or time spent working while away from work. In particular, time spent commuting to work is not treated as time devoted to work. Aguiar and Hurst define two different measures of market work. The first is what they call core market work, which simply includes time spent at work plus time devoted to work while away from work, either at home or elsewhere. As just noted, this measure of work corresponds most closely to the measure of market work that is used in standard data sets. The second is a variable called total market work, which includes time spent commuting to work.

Some categories of time use are not easily classified as either leisure or home production. At one extreme, categories such as doing dishes and doing laundry seem clear examples of home production. At the other extreme are activities such as watching TV or playing sports, which seem to be clear examples of leisure. But there are some intermediate categories for which classification is more difficult. Shopping is one example—going to the grocery store may be seen as home production rather than leisure, but a trip to the shopping mall may be a leisure activity for some. And child care may in some instances be viewed as home production, but may also be viewed as leisure.

In order to deal with the reality of murky boundaries, Aguiar and Hurst present a hierarchy of categories of time devoted to home production. They begin with a category called "core home production," which includes those activities for which there seems little controversy—meal preparation and cleanup, laundry, ironing, dusting, vacuuming, indoor household cleaning, and indoor design and maintenance (including painting and decorating). A second category includes time spent acquiring goods and services (excluding health care, education, and restaurant meals). Examples include grocery shopping, shopping for other household items, comparison shopping, coupon clipping, going to the bank, going to the barber, going to the post office, or buying goods on-line. A third category, denoted by "other homework," includes home maintenance, outdoor cleaning, vehicle repair, gardening, and pet care. Finally, Aguiar and Hurst also measure time devoted to child care.

We can create a hierarchy of measures of time devoted to home production by deciding which of these categories to include in our measure. In table 4-1 below I reproduce the results reported in Aguiar and Hurst for these various measures:

TABLE 4-1
WEEKLY HOURS BY TASK PER ADULT

	1965	1975	1985	1993	2003
Core Market	29.63	28.79	27.74	29.93	28.63
Total Market	35.98	33.79	32.67	33.22	31.71
Core Home Production	13.02	11.34	10.82	8.75	8.66
Shopping	6.18	5.40	5.84	5.20	5.19
Other	2.89	3.41	4.34	4.45	4.56
Core HP+Shopping	19.20	16.74	16.66	13.95	13.85
Core HP+Shopping+Other	22.09	20.15	21.00	18.40	18.31
Child Care	3.67	3.11	3.64	3.11	5.50

SOURCE: Aguiar and Hurst 2007a.
NOTE: HP = home production.

Note that the first line of this table, for core market work, looks fairly similar to the patterns that we saw earlier. In particular, there is a decrease from 1965 to 1985 of a little more than 6 percent. This is followed by a sharp increase in hours between 1985 and 1993, with hours in 1993 being higher than in 1965. There is then a decrease between 1993 and 2003. Since 2003 is in fact the low point of hours worked associated with the recession in 2001, this value should be interpreted appropriately. In our earlier data, hours worked in 2005 were almost 5 percent higher than in 2003. This table shows a decrease in market work between 1965 and 2003, but if we keep in mind that 2003 is the bottom of the recession in terms of hours worked, then the data are consistent with an overall small increase in hours worked between the beginning and end of the period, with the increase being on the order of 1 or 2 percent. So this is broadly consistent with our previous data.

Now we turn to the new information, showing the change in time devoted to home production. As the table shows, there has been a steady decrease in core home-production time between 1965 and 1993, with relatively little change in the last ten-year period covered by the table. Overall, the decrease is roughly four and a half hours per week. Next consider the remaining two categories: "shopping" and "other." While shopping time has decreased somewhat over the full period, the largest drop occurred in the first ten-year period. After that time there has been relatively little change overall. The category called "other" has actually shown an increase over the entire period, but most of it has come in the period 1965–1985.

The next two rows in the table show that in terms of the pattern of change in time devoted to home production, there is not that much difference between the various measures: the overall drop is 4.36 hours for core home production, versus 5.35 and 3.78 for the other two measures.

The final row of the table, which shows time devoted to child care, indicates relatively little change for the period 1965–1993. There are some small fluctuations, but they represent basically half an hour a week. From 1993 to 2003 there is a large increase in time devoted to child care, of more than two hours per week. This change is most likely due to differences between the ATUS and earlier surveys; 2003 was the first year that the ATUS was conducted, and one of its objectives was to measure time devoted to child care. The new survey allowed individuals to list activities carried out simultaneously as primary and secondary activities, so, for example, one could list cooking as a primary activity and child care as a secondary activity. The result of devoting more attention to measuring time allocated to child care was, predictably, to show more time allocated to child care than previous studies.

Given the relative constancy of time devoted to child care over the previous twenty-eight-year period, the increase from 1993 to 2003 is best interpreted as due to change in survey design. Given the change in survey design, my interpretation of the data is that the reduction in time devoted to home production is basically unaffected by whether we include child care in the measure of home production.

So far we have focused only on the aggregate data for time allocated across various activities. I argued earlier that the big change that occurred during this period involved the reallocation of time from home production to market production for women. It is therefore instructive to examine the same changes for men and women separately. This is done in the two panels of table 4-2.

TABLE 4-2

WEEKLY HOURS BY TASK PER ADULT: MEN VS. WOMEN

A. Men

	1965	1975	1985	1993	2003
Core Market	42.09	39.80	36.86	38.52	35.54
Total Market	51.58	46.53	43.35	42.74	39.53
Core Home Production	1.96	2.01	3.82	2.90	3.40
Shopping	4.85	4.44	4.59	3.83	4.34
Other	2.86	4.40	5.55	5.71	5.69
Core HP+Shopping	6.81	6.45	8.41	6.73	7.74
Core HP+Shopping +Other	9.67	10.85	13.96	12.44	13.43
Child Care	1.44	1.40	1.66	1.47	3.24

B. Women

	1965	1975	1985	1993	2003
Core Market	18.83	19.24	19.84	22.49	22.65
Total Market	22.45	22.74	23.41	24.97	24.93
Core Home Production	22.61	19.43	16.89	13.83	13.23
Shopping	7.33	6.23	6.92	6.38	5.93
Other	2.92	2.55	3.29	3.35	3.39
Core HP+Shopping	29.94	25.66	23.81	20.21	19.16
Core HP+Shopping+Other	32.86	28.21	27.10	23.56	22.55
Child Care	5.60	4.60	5.36	4.54	7.46

SOURCE: Aguiar and Hurst 2007a.
NOTE: HP = home production.

This table confirms the very different changes that have taken place for men and women. For men there has been a large decrease in market work and a small increase in time devoted to home production. The net result is a relatively large increase in leisure. For women, on the other hand, we see that there is a large decrease in time devoted to home production, and a smaller yet substantial increase in time devoted to market work. Once again, the net result is a sizable increase in leisure time.

Reassessing the Relationship between Labor Taxes and Market Work

Now that we have documented the patterns in the data, we can use the data to obtain a better estimate of the response of market work to changes in labor taxes. The problem we face is that the data consist of the composite of (at least) two effects: one is the response to changes in taxes, and the other is the response associated with the underlying force leading women to devote more time to market work as opposed to home production. The proposed solution is to basically extract the increase in total hours of market work that were associated with the movement of women into the labor force. To do this we compute the drop in time devoted to home production between 1965 and each of the subsequent years in the sample, and then deduct this many hours of market work from the market work category.[5]

This is a simple procedure designed to remove from the data the effect of increased female labor force participation. Each different measure of home-production time will yield a slightly different correction. Table 4-3 shows the resulting measures for market work based on three different measures of home-production time.

TABLE 4-3

MARKET WORK CORRECTED FOR CHANGES IN HOME PRODUCTION
(weekly hours per adult)

	1965	1975	1985	1993	2003
Original	29.63	28.79	27.74	29.93	28.63
Corrected 1	29.63	27.11	25.54	25.66	24.27
Corrected 2	29.63	26.33	25.20	24.68	23.28
Corrected 3	29.63	26.85	26.65	26.64	24.85

SOURCES: Aguiar and Hurst 2007a and author's calculation.

FIGURE 4–2

WEEKLY HOURS OF WORK, 1965–2003

(adjusted for 2001 recession)

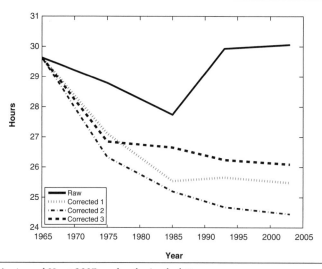

SOURCES: Aguiar and Hurst 2007a and author's calculations.

As noted earlier, the fact that 2003 is the low point of hours worked associated with the 2001 recession will necessarily magnify the extent of the decrease from 1965 to 2003. To correct for this, it is perhaps advisable to adjust the 2003 figure upward. In figure 4-2 I plot the four curves, but with an upward adjustment of 5 percent for the 2003 entries.

There are some minor differences among the three different corrections, but the most important feature is that in all three cases the basic pattern is a sharp drop between 1965 and 1975 or 1985, followed by a small decline after 1985. Overall, there is a relatively large drop from the beginning of the period to the end of the period, with the drop in all three cases exceeding 10 percent. Note that none of the corrected curves shows the rise of hours during the 1990s that were evident in figure 3-9. The reason for this is that we have no data points between 1993 and 2003, and therefore are missing the period associated with the large increase in hours.

Having constructed a series for hours of work that purges the data of the changes associated with the increased labor force participation of women, we can now revisit the issue of what the data have to say about the effects of increasing labor taxes on overall hours of work. Comparing figure 4-2 for hours with figure 3-1 for taxes on labor, we can see a significant negative effect of labor tax rates on hours of work. In terms of magnitudes, the change in taxes is on the order of 8 or 9 percent, and the drop in hours is on the order of 15 percent, suggesting that each 1 percent increase in taxes leads to a decrease in hours worked of about 1.5 percent.

Summary

The simplest look at the time series changes in hours of work and tax rates in the United States suggests no strong relationship between hours worked and labor tax rates. If we examine the relationship over different subperiods, we see that the period 1956–1975 is consistent with such a relationship, but the later period is not. Second, the U.S. time series is not necessarily a good source for uncovering the effect of labor taxes on hours of work, since the changes in hours of work associated with the massive increase in female labor force participation dominate the effects of tax changes. Third, when we adjust the data to take into account the large movement from home production to market work associated with the increase in female labor force participation, we find evidence in support of a substantial negative relationship between tax rates on labor and hours worked.

5

What We Learn from the Experience of Other Countries

In the last chapter I reviewed the evidence from aggregate time series data for the United States and argued that a simple look at the relationship between aggregate hours of work and tax rates does not suggest any significant negative effect of tax rates on hours of work. But I went on to argue that this simple look is misleading. The true relationship is obscured by the relatively small size of the change in labor tax rates in the United States, so that the effects of tax changes on hours worked are masked by those of another large change that occurred during the same time period: the movement from home production to market production associated with the dramatic increase in women in the workforce. I then argued that one does find evidence for significant negative effects of higher tax rates on labor supply if one uses data on time spent in home production to control for the underlying changes in time allocation between home production and market production.

We would not need to carry out these adjustments to the data to uncover the effects of taxes if the change in taxes in the United States over the last fifty or so years had been large relative to other changes that were also taking place. This observation tells us that to confirm the inference that higher tax rates have a negative effect on labor supply, we should look for cases with sustained increases in tax rates that are much larger than those found in the United States. It turns out that we can easily find such increases in the experiences of other OECD countries.

Labor Taxes in the OECD

Table 5-1 shows the effective average tax rate on labor in several OECD countries in 1960, 1980, and 2000. In each case the value is the average for a five-year interval centered on the year in question. The source for these tax rates is McDaniel (2006), and they are constructed using the method described in chapter 3 for the United States.

TABLE 5-1
AVERAGE EFFECTIVE TAX RATES ON LABOR INCOME
IN SELECTED OECD COUNTRIES

	1960	1980	2000	Change 1960–2000
Australia	15.8%	24.6%	27.2%	11.4
Austria	31.3	43.6	48.5	17.2
Belgium	29.0	43.6	50.0	21.0
Canada	20.7	28.5	36.0	15.3
Finland	26.0	40.4	52.4	26.4
France	36.6	43.7	49.7	13.1
Germany	33.5	43.4	47.7	14.2
Italy	25.5	33.2	49.1	23.6
Japan	18.4	23.4	30.5	12.1
Netherlands	32.1	49.2	45.1	13.0
Spain	16.0	24.4	35.6	19.6
Sweden	31.6	53.9	59.1	27.5
Switzerland	17.3	25.1	32.7	15.4
United Kingdom	25.7	36.1	36.0	10.3
United States	22.1	26.4	28.6	6.5
Average	**25.4%**	**36.0%**	**41.9%**	**16.5**

SOURCE: McDaniel 2006.

The last row of this table is striking—it shows that in terms of averages, tax rates on labor increased by more than sixteen percentage points over this time period, almost three times the increase that was observed in the United States. In fact, the United States was the only country to have an increase that was less than ten percentage points. Some countries even had increases in excess of twenty percentage points. The table also shows that these increases have been sustained, since almost two-thirds of the overall increase takes place during the first twenty-year period. It follows that other countries are much more likely to provide a cleaner look at the effects of higher tax rates on aggregate hours of work.

Hours Worked in the OECD

Using the same data that were used to construct figure 3-9 for hours worked in the United States, table 5-2 shows hours worked in 1960, 1980, and 2000 for the same set of countries as table 5-1.

TABLE 5-2
WEEKLY HOURS WORKED PER PERSON AGED 15–64
IN SELECTED OECD COUNTRIES

	1960	1980	2000	% Change 1960–2000
Australia	25.1	23.7	24.0	−4.3
Austria	28.8	22.5	22.7	−21.1
Belgium	25.8	18.7	18.3	−29.2
Canada	22.8	22.8	23.8	4.6
Finland	32.0	25.8	22.2	−30.7
France	29.8	23.2	19.3	−35.3
Germany	28.7	21.9	19.8	−30.9
Italy	31.2	20.5	21.2	−32.3
Japan	33.2	30.1	26.4	−20.5
Netherlands	26.6	20.1	20.5	−22.7
Spain	23.1	19.4	19.5	−15.5
Sweden	25.3	23.0	23.5	−7.0
Switzerland	32.4	27.2	27.0	−16.7
United Kingdom	32.7	26.5	23.3	−28.8
United States	23.7	23.4	26.0	10.0
Average	**28.1**	**23.3**	**22.5**	**−18.7**

SOURCES: Hours from GGDC (http://www.conference-board.org/economics/database.cfm); population from OECD (http://stats.oecd.org/index.aspx?r=861732).
NOTES: For 1980 and 2000, the value is the average over a five-year interval centered on 1980 and 2000, respectively. Because data are only available from 1960 onward for some countries, the 1960 value is an average over the period 1960–62.

These data are interesting in and of themselves, and so it is worthwhile to take some time to discuss the patterns that they exhibit. Let's begin by looking at what happened to the average value for hours worked. What we see is that hours worked decreased dramatically from 1960 to 1980, followed by a small decrease thereafter. The overall drop in hours from the beginning to the end of the period is more than 18 percent. This is an enormous drop in hours worked. Consider by way of comparison the labor market fluctuations associated with the business cycle. Going from normal times to a fairly severe recession is usually associated with a drop in total hours worked of about 3 percent. The size of the average drop that we see across countries is more than six times as large. So this drop in hours worked over time is something very dramatic.

The second striking pattern in these data is the dramatic differences in the overall change in hours worked across countries. At one extreme is the United States, which actually witnessed an increase of 10 percent between these two dates, and at the other extreme are Germany and France, with declines of more than 30 percent. If we contrast the differential changes between the United States and France, the difference is staggering—more than 45 percent.

While the United States is at one extreme, it is important to note that it is not an outlier. Canada also displayed substantial growth in hours of work, and Australia had only a very small decrease. Moreover, even among those countries that exhibited substantial decreases in hours worked, there is still a lot of variation. Switzerland, for example, had a decrease in hours worked of 17 percent, which is much less than what occurred in France, Germany, and Belgium.

Changes in Taxes and Changes in Hours of Work

Before we put together the two key pieces of data, the changes in labor taxes and the changes in hours worked, we should ask whether increased female labor force participation does not also obscure the evidence in these OECD countries.[1] In fact, the pattern of increasing labor force participation of women is a trend in all of the countries in the above table. However, there are two key points to note, relating to a direct and indirect effect of changes in labor taxes. The direct effect corresponds to the fact that even if this underlying force influences all economies, it presents less of an interpretive problem if the change in labor tax rates is larger. This is because the problem occurs precisely when the change in market hours due to whatever force is driving the increased female labor force participation is large relative to the change in hours associated with the change in taxes. But if the change in taxes is much larger, as it is in countries other than the United States, this is less of a concern.

The indirect effect derives from a point made in the last chapter about the model including home production. Specifically, in such a model an increase in taxes on labor creates an incentive for individuals to perform more activities for themselves rather than purchasing them in the market. For example, high tax rates increase the incentives for individuals to cook meals at home rather than going to restaurants, to paint their own house instead of hiring someone to paint it for them, or to take care of children or elderly family members rather than purchase these services in the market. In fact, a study by Davis and Henrekson (2004) looks at data for several OECD countries and shows that countries with higher tax rates tend to have much less market activity in exactly those activities for which there are good nonmarket substitutes.

This implies that increases in taxes tend to dampen the effects associated with the underlying force that leads more women to engage in market work.[2] The bottom line is that a country with a greater increase in labor taxes will tend to have larger effects on hours worked associated with the direct effect of the tax changes, while the changes associated with the underlying force leading more women to engage in more market work will be dampened by the indirect effect. Both effects imply that the pure response of hours to taxes will be more apparent in the data if the change in taxes are larger.

We can now examine what the data say about the effect of changes in labor taxes on hours of work. It is instructive to begin with a look at what happened to the simple averages across countries for both labor taxes and hours worked. Between 1960 and 2000 the labor tax rate increases by 16.5 percentage points, and hours of work decrease by 18.7 percent. This suggests a strong negative effect of taxes on hours of work. For the reasons noted in the case of the United States, it is likely that the effect is even stronger than this suggests, since the average includes countries such as the United States, where the large reallocation of home-to-market production is present.

While it is interesting to look at the averages, a more powerful test is to examine the pattern of changes across countries. That is, to what extent do countries with larger increases in taxes also have larger decreases in hours worked? Figure 5-1 provides a graphical look at the relationship. It plots the data for changes in tax rates and percentage change in hours of work for each of the fifteen countries. The picture shows a clear negative relationship: the correlation between the change in tax rate and the percentage change in hours of work is equal to –0.30.[3]

FIGURE 5-1

CHANGES IN HOURS AND LABOR TAXES
IN 15 OECD COUNTRIES, 1960–2000

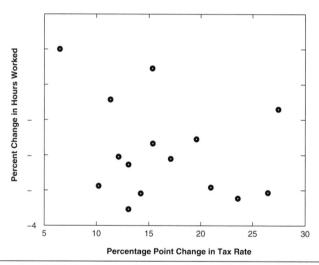

SOURCES: Hours from GGDC (http://www.conference-board.org/economics/database.cfm); population from OECD (http://stats.oecd.org/index.aspx?r=861732); McDaniel 2006 (for taxes).

Another way to represent this information is to run a simple regression of the percentage change in hours of work on change in tax rate:

$$\log(h_{i2000}) - \log(h_{i1960}) = a(\tau_{i2000} - \tau_{i1960}) + \varepsilon_i,$$

where h_i is hours worked in year t in country i, and τ_i is the labor tax in country i in year t. The result of this regression is a coefficient of –1.27 on the change in tax rates, implying that if tax rates increase by ten percentage points, then hours of work will decrease by 12.1 percent.

Recall that the estimate for the United States in the previous chapter, based on the data that were purged of the effects of increased female labor force participation, implied a drop of hours of about 15 percent in response to a 10 percent increase in tax rates. Noting that this current estimate is likely biased downward because these data have not been purged of the effect of increased female labor force participation, I conclude that the cross-country evidence is essentially in line with the earlier estimates.

Cultural Differences

If we look at the data shown for the year 2000 in table 5-2, we see that hours worked are lowest in the continental European economies of Belgium, France, Germany, and Italy, are at intermediate levels in the UK, Finland, and Sweden, and are the highest in the United States, Canada, Australia, Japan, and Switzerland. Many commentators are content to explain away these differences as being due to cultural differences; the idea is that people from some countries either enjoy leisure more or are less focused on work.

This view leads some people to argue that U.S. policymakers should not look to these other countries for information about how tax policies influence hours of work. They would argue that many Europeans work less than Americans not because of high taxes on labor and generous transfer systems, but instead because of systematically different preferences toward work and consumption across countries.

A closer look at the data suggests that this is not a very compelling explanation. In 1960, hours of work were actually higher in Germany, France, and Belgium than they were in Canada, the United States, and Australia. That is, fifty years ago the relative work levels of these countries were reversed. This evidence seems inconsistent with the view that Europeans work less because they either value leisure more or do not care so much about consumption.

Since that time, hours have increased somewhat in the United States but decreased dramatically in most European countries. The question is why. Something has changed in Europe relative to the United States that has led to these very different changes in the amount of work being done. I conclude, based on the above analysis, that the dominant force behind these very different changes is the relative changes in the rate at which labor is taxed.

Moreover, the way I have examined the data actually allows for the possibility that Europeans have different attitudes about how much they want to work. To see why, it is important to note that the above estimates of tax effects did not come from comparing the relative level of work in Europe with the relative level of labor taxes in Europe. That comparison would in principle mistakenly attribute differences that might be due to preferences to differences in taxes. Instead, the above analysis focused entirely on comparing the changes in work in each country with the changes in taxes in that same country. In a country where people like to work a lot, for whatever reason, this preference will manifest itself as higher hours worked in both 1960 and 2000, and hence does not affect the change in hours between these two dates. Similarly, in a country in which people prefer not to work so much, this preference will manifest itself as lower hours of work in both 1960 and 2000. Once again, this has no bearing on the change in hours between 1960 and 2000.

Other Explanations for Differences in Hours Worked

The evidence just presented shows that there is a strong negative correlation between changes in hours worked and changes in labor taxes in a sample of fifteen OECD countries. I have interpreted this as evidence in support of the notion that the changes in taxes were the source of the changes in hours worked in these countries. But it is still possible that the changes in hours worked might be due to some other change going on at the same time as the changes in labor taxes, and that we are mistaken in claiming that the change in hours of work is due to taxes.

An example will help to illustrate the point. It is well known that the economies of continental Europe differ from the U.S. economy in several respects other than taxes. For example, these economies tend to have more-regulated labor markets, including stricter employment protection policies that make it difficult for firms to adjust their workforce downward. Many researchers argue that such policies lower the incentives for firms to hire workers, thereby adversely affecting total hours of work. Unions are also more prevalent in these economies, and many researchers argue that unions adopt policies that have negative consequences for overall employment and hours of work.

Thus it is plausible that at the same time that these economies were increasing their taxes on labor, they might also have been increasing the degree of employment protection and increasing the role of unions. After all, transfer payments, employment protection, and greater union presence are typically viewed as common aspects of the European welfare state. So maybe it is changes in employment protection or unionization that are driving the changes in hours worked, and we are incorrectly interpreting these changes as being due to increases in taxes, simply because we have not looked for changes in these other factors. Below I deal with this critique.

To be sure, no matter how many explanations one rejects regarding the decline in hours worked in these other countries, it will always be possible to imagine yet another one. As I noted in chapter 2, at any point in time there are countless small changes going on in any given economy. It follows that if we are trying to come up with plausible stories about changes that might account for a small change in hours worked, there are presumably many stories that we would have to consider. But if the changes in hours worked are very large, then we need to come up with some large changes that took place in the economy, and there are typically many fewer large changes going on at any point in time. Recall from the data presented in the previous section that in some economies, hours worked decreased by more than 30 percent between 1960 and 2000. If we are trying to understand what might account for this, it stands to reason that we can focus our attention on big changes in the economy.

It turns out that it is quite difficult to come up with examples of big changes in the fifteen economies at issue that have the right qualitative pattern, i.e., that changed much more in countries like France than in the United States. What I want to do in this section is show that other differences, such as unionization or employment protection, do not seem to fit the pattern.

I begin with a study of unionization as a potential alternative explanation. Recall that if we go back to 1960, then hours of work in many European countries exceed those in the United States. The key change over time is that hours of work have progressively decreased in many European countries, up through the late 1980s, at which point they level off. On the other hand, the unionization rate in Europe is basically constant over time. So if the higher rate of unionization in Europe is the current cause of the lower hours of work in Europe as compared to the United States, we are left with a major puzzle—why is it that these same higher unionization rates were not associated with lower hours of work forty or fifty years ago?

Figure 5-2 shows the evolution of unionization rates among two groups of countries—those with high hours of work in 2000 and those with low hours of work in 2000.[4] The figure is quite revealing. In the European countries, there is an increase in unionization rates between 1960 and 1975, but subsequently the level decreases, so that in 1995 the level is almost unchanged from 1970. Moreover, the figure also shows that there is relatively little difference in unionization rates across the two sets of economies.

FIGURE 5-2

EVOLUTION OF UNIONIZATION RATES AMONG COUNTRIES
WITH HIGH VS. LOW HOURS OF WORK IN 2000

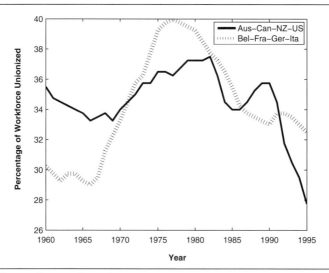

SOURCE: Alesina, Glaeser, and Sacerdote 2005.

This last comparison is perhaps subject to some debate, since there are two different measures of unionization that economists sometimes look at. One is union density, which is what is reported above. Union density measures the fraction of workers who are union members. A second measure is union coverage, which instead measures the fraction of workers whose wages are governed by union agreements. In some European countries, such as France, the norm is for wages negotiated by unions to also apply to nonunion workers. Using this second measure can make unions seem more important in some of these European countries. But in fact, even if one uses this alternative measure, it remains true that unionization has changed relatively little in Europe over the post-1960 period.[5] The bottom line is that it is difficult see any evidence that differences in unions are responsible for the very different dynamics of hours worked across countries.

Next I consider the case of employment protection. Measuring employment protection policies is not entirely straightforward. There are many different components to these policies, including such things as the amount of advance notice required to lay off workers, the size of required severance payments, procedures required for collective dismissals, and restrictions concerning hiring of temporary workers. Each of these is in turn characterized by several different components, since, for example, severance pay typically is a function of how many years a worker has been employed at a given establishment. These measurement issues notwithstanding, various researchers have constructed indices to measure the extent of these regulations, both over time and across countries. In what follows I report results that rely on the measures used by Alesina, Glaeser, and Sacerdote (2005), although I draw different conclusions than they do.

For each year between 1960 and 1995, each country is assigned an index between 0 and 2 to indicate the severity of its employment protection regulations, with 0 indicating the least stringent and 2 indicating the most stringent. To give some sense of the variation, the United States is the country with the lowest average value for this index, being equal to 0.1 in all years. At the other extreme, Italy is the country with the highest average value of the index, with a value of 1.96.

A first look at these data might suggest an important role for employment protection in accounting for the very different behavior of total hours worked across countries. Consider the time series for the average of the employment protection index across the same fifteen countries that appeared in tables 5-1 and 5-2, which is shown in figure 5-3. This index shows a steady increase from the early 1960s to the mid-1970s, and is then relatively constant until the mid-1980s, at which point it declines. As of 1995 this index is about the same as it was in the early 1970s. Because the period from the early 1960s to the mid-1970s was a period in which average hours of work also declined, the above figure would suggest a potentially important role for employment protection in accounting for this pattern. On the other hand, the fact that this index in 1995 is at the same level as in the early 1970s is sharply at odds with the fact that hours worked in 1995 (or even later, if one wants to allow for some lagged response) are still dramatically lower than in the early 1970s.

FIGURE 5-3
AVERAGE EMPLOYMENT PROTECTION INDEX

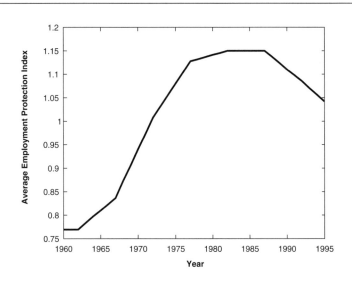

SOURCE: Alesina, Glaeser, and Sacerdote 2005.

Although this evidence already strongly suggests that employment protection is not the key force behind the large declines in hours worked in many countries, it is still interesting to look at the data for some individual countries. The average value of this index for the four countries with the lowest hours worked in 1995 (Belgium, France, Germany, and Italy) is 1.47, whereas the average for the countries with the highest hours of work (Australia, Canada, New Zealand, and the United States) is 0.43. This would seem to suggest that the presence of stringent employment protection measures may be an important factor in accounting for differences in hours of work. Moreover, it turns out that the index increased from 0.83 to 1.47 for the four European countries between 1960 and 1995, whereas it was unchanged for the other four economies. This also suggests that the increase in employment protection measures in these European economies may be an important factor in accounting for the decline in hours of work in their economies relative to the other four economies.

But a closer look at the experiences of individual countries shows us that changes in employment protection most likely do not explain the key patterns found in the data. To see why, we look at the changes over time in some specific countries. Figure 5-4 shows the employment protection index over time for three European countries: France, Germany, and Italy. The figure reveals some important differences in how employment protection has changed in the three countries. Italy had virtually no change over this period except for a gradual decline in the last ten years of the period. In contrast, both France and Germany experienced large increases in the level of this

FIGURE 5-4

EMPLOYMENT PROTECTION INDEX IN THREE EUROPEAN COUNTRIES, 1960–1995

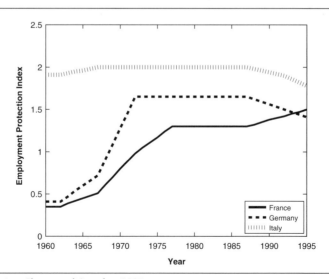

SOURCE: Alesina, Glaeser, and Sacerdote 2005.

index, with the extent of the increase being roughly the same in each country. But whereas Germany experienced all of the increase by 1970, with a small decline after 1985, France experienced a gradual increase through the mid-seventies and a further gradual increase after 1985.

Given the differences in the size of the increases and the timing of those increases, we would expect that if employment protection were the key factor behind the changes in hours worked in these countries, we would see evidence of this in the changes in hours worked over time as well. Figure 5-5 shows the time series for weekly hours worked per person aged fifteen to sixty-four for these three countries over the same period. The most salient feature of this picture is the similarity of the changes in hours worked across countries. In particular, all three countries experience relatively constant declines in hours of work from 1960 through the mid-1980s and are relatively constant after that. The constancy of the index for Italy relative to the other two countries does not seem to manifest itself at all in dramatically different behavior for hours worked. Nor does the different behavior for France and Germany show up as differences in the series for hours of work.

FIGURE 5-5

WEEKLY HOURS WORKED IN THREE EUROPEAN COUNTRIES, 1960–2003
(per person aged 15–64)

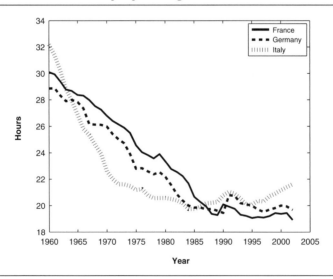

SOURCE: Hours from GGDC (http://www.conference-board.org/economics/database.cfm); population from OECD (http://stats.oecd.org/index.aspx?r=861732).

In fact, the changes for other countries are even more dramatic. Consider the case of Austria. Between 1960 and 1995 Austria experiences a decrease in hours of work equal to almost 25 percent, as shown in figure 5-6.

FIGURE 5-6

WEEKLY HOURS WORKED IN AUSTRIA, 1960–2003

(per person aged 15–64)

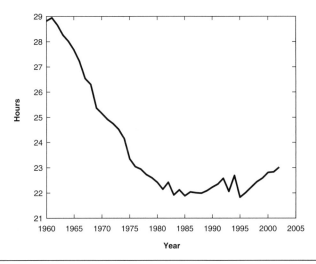

SOURCES: Hours from GGDC (http://www.conference-board.org/economics/database.cfm); population from OECD (http://stats.oecd.org/index.aspx?r=861732).

The dynamics for the employment protection index in Austria are shown in figure 5-7. The index displays no change until after 1970, but the great majority of the decrease in hours worked has already occurred at this point.

To summarize, while a first pass at the data presented in figure 5-3 suggests that employment protection might be an important factor in accounting for the changes in hours worked across countries, a closer look at the data indicates that employment protection cannot be a very important factor in accounting for the overall decline in hours of work in European countries relative to the United States.

My goal in presenting the evidence on unions and employment protection was to show that these other explanations do not really pass a simple eyeball test; a look at the time series changes on a graph makes

FIGURE 5-7

EMPLOYMENT PROTECTION INDEX IN AUSTRIA, 1960–1995

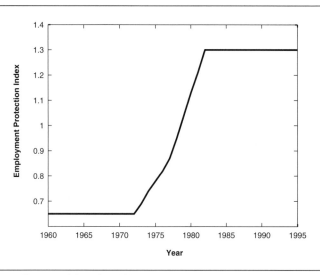

SOURCE: Alesina, Glaeser, and Sacerdote 2005.

very clear how unconvincing these alternative explanations are. This view is supported by more formal statistical evidence. Ohanian, Raffo, and Rogerson (2008) run a regression of log hours worked on tax rates and several other factors, including employment protection and unionization rates, and find that only taxes account for a substantial share in the drop in hours worked.

Supporting Evidence: Home versus Market Production

There is yet other evidence that higher taxes are largely responsible for the significant differences in hours worked across countries. In this section I consider some related evidence that has to do with cross-country differences in time devoted to household production.

In chapter 4 I described how to extend the standard model of labor supply to include an additional use of time, labeled home production. In discussing the effects of labor taxes in this extended framework I emphasized that an important additional channel was now present. Specifically, if taxes increase, this creates an incentive for individuals to do more things for themselves rather than purchase them in the market. The intuition is simple: if you are working to purchase something in the market, then higher taxes imply that you have to work more hours in order to earn enough money to make the purchase. Since time spent in home production is not taxed, higher taxes serve to make it more economical to do things for oneself rather than purchasing them through the market.

It follows that, holding all else constant, we should expect to see more time devoted to home production in an economy with a higher tax rate on labor than in an economy with a lower tax rate. And if the effects of taxes are sizable, then these differences should also be sizable. In chapter 4 I reported data showing how time allocated to home production has changed over time in the United States. Unfortunately, the data that would permit a cross-country comparison of time series changes in home production are not available. However, four recent papers look at available time-use data to provide a recent snapshot of how time devoted to market and home production differs across some countries.

A common finding is that differences in market work are indeed significantly offset by differences in home production. Freeman and Schettkat (2001) study time allocation data for married couples in Germany and the United States in the 1990s and find that Americans devote more time to market work and less time to home production than do Germans. The striking finding is about total time devoted to work (i.e., market work plus home production): it turns out that the two countries are virtually the same. This study also shows that the patterns of consumer expenditure differ in a corresponding fashion; i.e., Germans spend more time on meal preparation at home and spend less money at eating establishments.

Freeman and Schettkat (2005) extend this analysis to a larger set of countries and report that as of the early 1990s, time spent in home production in European countries is about 20 percent higher than in the United States. This implies that increased time in home production only partially offsets the decrease in time devoted to market work.

Using data from the recent Harmonised European Time Use Study, Ragan (2005) compares several European countries with the United States and finds that on average, individuals in Belgium, France, Germany, Italy, and the

Netherlands devote between 15 and 20 percent more time to home production than do Americans.[6]

In another study of time-use data, Burda, Hamermesh, and Weil (2008) reach a similar conclusion based on information for Germany, Italy, the Netherlands, and the United States. In particular, they find that Europeans spend 15–20 percent more time in home production than do Americans.[7]

Related work (described earlier) has also been carried out by Davis and Henrekson (2004). Consistent with the tax effects on home versus market production discussed above, they show that countries with higher marginal tax rates systematically have lower employment in those market activities for which there are good nonmarket substitutes. The magnitude of the estimated effects is large. An increase in taxes of one quarter of one percent leads to a decrease equal to 2.4 percent in the employment share in the broad set of sectors that have good home-produced substitutes. They find that tax effects are most noticeable in precisely these sectors.

The Netherlands

In the final section of this chapter I take a closer look at the time series changes in hours worked and taxes in the Netherlands. The Netherlands turns out to be the only country in our sample that has experienced both a persistent increase in taxes and a persistent decrease in taxes. All of the other countries have persistent increases in taxes, and differ from one another only in the extent of the increase. My previous analysis has shown that those countries with the largest increases in taxes also tended to have the largest declines in hours of work. But there would be a stronger case for taxes as the dominant factor behind these decreases in hours if there was also evidence that decreases in taxes lead to increases in hours worked.

But while we have examples in the data that allow us to compare economies that have increased taxes by different amounts, the only instance of a persistent decline in tax rates is in the Netherlands. Figure 5-8 shows the trend behavior of the average labor tax rate for the Netherlands.

We can see that the Netherlands has a large and sustained increase in taxes for roughly the first twenty-five years of the sample, followed by a smaller but still substantial and sustained decrease in tax rates over the final twenty years.

Figure 5-9 presents the time series behavior of hours worked in the Netherlands. It shows a dramatic and sustained decrease over the first part of the sample, followed by a smaller but sustained increase in the later part of the period. The increase in hours begins about five years after the decrease in tax rates, but given that there is some noise in the tax rate measures, this lag of five years should not be taken too literally; the actual maximum value of the tax rate occurred in 1983. The fact that there is some lag between the tax changes and the response in hours is consistent with ideas that we emphasized earlier, including the point that there needs to be sufficient time following a tax change for the effects to take place. In any case, the time series changes for taxes and hours of work in the Netherlands seem very persuasive evidence regarding the effect of taxes on

FIGURE 5-8

AVERAGE LABOR TAX RATE IN THE NETHERLANDS, 1956–2003

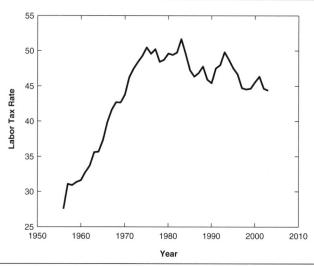

Year

SOURCE: McDaniel 2006.

FIGURE 5-9

WEEKLY HOURS OF WORK IN THE NETHERLANDS, 1960–2003

(per person aged 15–64)

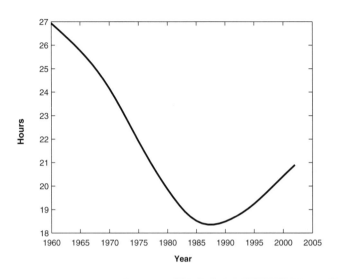

SOURCES: Hours from GGDC (http://www.conference-board.org/economics/database.cfm); population from OECD (http://stats.oecd.org/index.aspx?r=861732).

hours of work: just as tax increases have a negative effect on hours worked, tax decreases seem to have a positive effect.

Summary

This chapter has argued that data from countries other than the United States are likely to contain much better information on the effect of increases in labor taxes on hours worked. The reason for this is that labor taxes have increased much more in these other countries than in the United States. Whereas the changes in the United States are not large enough to dominate other effects during the same time period, in many other countries the tax changes are as much as three times larger. When we compare outcomes across countries, we find sharp evidence that greater increases in labor taxes lead to greater decreases in hours of work.

These changes in other countries are not likely to be due to changes in other policy or institutional factors, such as employment protection or unionization, or to cultural differences. Consistent with the notion that the changes in hours worked are primarily due to changes in taxes, we find that in countries with higher labor tax rates, individuals devote less time to market work and more time to home production.

6

Understanding Scandinavia

The key finding of previous chapters is that those countries that experienced higher increases in labor taxes also experienced larger decreases in hours of work. This evidence for the negative impact of taxes on hours of work, while straightforward and compelling, is not part of a true controlled experiment, and as a result cannot be deemed definitive. An important part of the process by which economists develop consensus on issues like this is to consider alternative explanations or evidence that seems inconsistent with a given explanation; if the former can be rebutted and the latter accounted for, then the original case becomes stronger. In the last chapter I addressed some alternative explanations for decreases in hours of work. In this chapter I want to address possible evidence against the finding that labor taxes have a significant effect on labor supply. This evidence comes from the Scandinavian countries of Denmark, Norway, and Sweden.

To see the evidence, let's go back to tables 5-1 and 5-2 in chapter 5. These two tables showed the level of labor taxes and hours of work for each of fifteen economies. In particular, let's take a look at the data for the year 2000. On the one hand it is true that if we compare European countries as a whole with, say, the United States, we see that labor taxes are higher in Europe and hours worked are lower. This is of course consistent with the findings I have emphasized. However, if we look more closely within the group of European countries, we see that Sweden has a tax rate that is almost ten percentage points higher than that of any other country, yet has hours of work that are roughly midway between those of continental Europe (i.e., Belgium, France, Germany, and Italy) and the United States. If indeed labor taxes exert such a negative effect on hours of work, how can it be that hours of work are so high in Sweden?

This is the question that I take up in this chapter. It turns out that the key to answering this question is to be found in a point made in chapter 2, that it is very important to take into account how governments spend the revenues generated from labor taxes in order to accurately predict the consequences for overall hours of work. I will show that Scandinavia is somewhat special in this regard.

The Importance of How the Government Spends

The tax data that I have used from McDaniel (2006) include Sweden but not Denmark or Norway. But since there are other studies that suggest that labor taxes in Denmark and Norway are comparable to those in Sweden, I will consider all three economies in my analysis here. Given that I do not have a consistent long time series on labor taxes, I will instead present data on current receipts of government relative to GDP. In chapter 3 I presented this series for the United States (figure 3-1), and we saw that it tracked the labor tax rate quite well. This is not surprising, since the reality is that most government revenue ultimately comes from labor.

Figures 6-1 and 6-2 show the time series for trend changes in both current receipts of government relative to GDP and weekly hours worked per person in employment for the two groups of economies: continental Europe (Belgium, France, Germany, and Italy) and Scandinavia (Denmark, Norway, and Sweden). These two figures clearly illustrate the potentially problematic evidence. As of 1960 these two sets of economies look virtually identical in terms of these two measures: current government receipts relative to GDP are a little above 30 percent, and weekly hours of work per person of working age are around 25.5. Both sets of countries experienced a large sustained increase in the size of government revenues over the next forty years, about fifteen percentage points in continental Europe and twenty-five percentage points in Scandinavia. And in both cases there was a large sustained decrease in hours of work, about 32 percent in continental Europe and 17 percent in Scandinavia.

What about the magnitudes of tax effects? If we take these two pieces of evidence separately, then the changes in continental Europe suggest that hours worked decrease by 2 percent for every 1 percent increase in the tax

FIGURE 6-1

CURRENT RECEIPTS OF GOVERNMENT AS A PERCENTAGE OF GDP IN
CONTINENTAL EUROPE AND SCANDINAVIA, 1960–2000

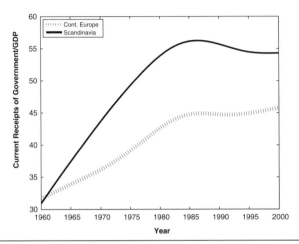

SOURCE: *OECD Historical Statistics* (Paris: OECD Publishing) for the years specified. Notes: Continental Europe = Belgium, France, Germany, and Italy. Scandinavia = Sweden, Denmark, and Norway.

FIGURE 6-2

WEEKLY HOURS WORKED IN CONTINENTAL EUROPE
AND SCANDINAVIA, 1960–2003

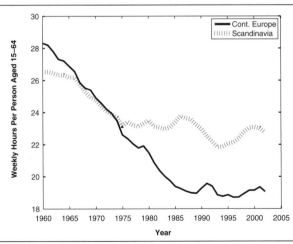

SOURCES: Hours from GGDC (http://www.conference-board.org/economics/database.cfm); population from OECD (http://stats.oecd.org/index.aspx?r=861732).
NOTE: Continental Europe = Belgium, France, Germany, and Italy. Scandinavia = Sweden, Denmark, and Norway.

rate, whereas the Scandinavian changes suggest that hours decrease by about three-quarters of a percent for each 1 percent increase in the tax rate. In both cases the effects are large. But at the same time the two estimates are quite different, with one of them being more than twice as large as the other.

This difference might lead us to question whether taxes are the driving force behind the change in hours worked in these countries. After all, if taxes are as important as the calculation for continental Europe suggests, then the decrease in hours worked in Scandinavia should have been almost 50 percent, rather than the 17 percent that we observed. We might infer either that this number is incorrect or that there is something else going on in Scandinavia that is also very important. If this something else is not related to taxes, then there are other things possibly even more important than taxes, in which case our evidence becomes somewhat less compelling.

Two differences between Scandinavia and continental Europe bear on this issue. The first has to do with potential differences in the amount of wasteful spending. The second has to do with the use of tax revenues to subsidize consumption. I know of no systematic attempts to measure cross-country differences in wasteful spending, or spending that does not provide anything of value to consumers. Many types of spending might in fact provide something of use, but if the spending is greater than is required to provide this utility, then the excess constitutes waste. A natural place to look for waste in terms of government spending on goods and services is in government employment. Hiring more workers than is necessary to provide a given service, adding unnecessary layers of bureaucracy, or duplicating administrative duties across agencies are all examples that constitute wasteful spending.

It is therefore of interest to examine differences in government employment across the two groups of economies. Table 6-1 shows government employment relative to the size of the working-age population in the two sets of countries, as well as in the United States as a reference point, for 1960, 1970, 1980, and 1993, which is the last data available for this series in the *OECD Historical Statistics*.

The table reveals several interesting patterns. First, the ratio of government employment to population aged fifteen to sixty-four has been basically constant in the United States. Second, and perhaps somewhat surprising, while the size of government employment relative to population has increased slightly over time in continental Europe, as of 1993 the size

TABLE 6-1

GOVERNMENT EMPLOYMENT AS A FRACTION OF POPULATION AGED 15–64

	1960	1970	1980	1993
Continental Europe	.07	.08	.09	.11
Scandinavia	.08	.12	.20	.23
United States	.10	.11	.11	.10

SOURCE: *OECD Historical Statistics* (Paris: OECD Publishing) for the years specified.
NOTES: Continental European countries are Belgium, France, Germany, and Italy. Scandinavian countries are Sweden, Denmark, and Norway.

of government employment relative to population is basically the same as in the United States. Recall that we are looking at the size of government employment relative to the population aged fifteen to sixty-four. Because the ratio of overall employment to population is lower in Europe than in the United States, it is true that the share of total employment accounted for by government is somewhat larger in continental Europe than it is in the United States. This share is 18.5 percent in Europe versus 14.5 percent in the United States.[1] In sharp contrast to the United States and continental Europe, the size of government in Scandinavia, as measured by employment, is almost one quarter of the population aged fifteen to sixty-four. Government employment as a share of total employment is almost 32 percent![2]

The second difference that I want to document has to do with the nature of government spending on goods and services. One of the distinctive features of the Scandinavian social welfare system is that the government spends a lot of money subsidizing family services, specifically child care and elderly care. Table 6-2 shows how this type of spending by the government differs across the three sets of countries. It is expressed as a fraction of total private consumption to better reflect the relative importance of these expenditures across these countries. These data are taken from Ragan (2005) and are averages for the years 1993–1996.

The table shows that there is a dramatic difference in this type of spending across the three sets of economies. Although the value is slightly higher in Europe than in the United States, once again one could summarize this table by saying that the United States and continental Europe are quite similar, whereas Scandinavia is dramatically different.

TABLE 6-2

GOVERNMENT SPENDING ON FAMILY SERVICES AS A
FRACTION OF PRIVATE CONSUMPTION, 1993–1996

Continental Europe	.014
Scandinavia	.080
United States	.00

SOURCE: Ragan 2005.
NOTES: Continental European countries are Belgium, France, Germany, and Italy. Scandinavian countries are Sweden, Denmark, and Norway.

To see why this type of spending is of particular importance, recall the home production model that I outlined in chapter 4. I argued that when taxes increase, we should expect individuals to respond by choosing to perform for themselves those services that are relatively easy to substitute for their market counterparts, such as cooking more meals at home, cleaning one's home and doing one's laundry, or painting one's house.

Child care and elderly care are also two very good examples of this type of service. So in an economy with high taxes, we would expect to see individuals perform more child care and elderly care outside of the market. But if the government uses tax revenues to subsidize the market provision of child care and elderly care, then the very services that were going to be forced out of the market because of the high taxes will be brought back in by the subsidies. The net result is that the taxes do not have the large disincentive effects on hours of market work that we would have otherwise expected.

One piece of evidence that is related to this effect has to do with employment rates by gender. Table 6-3 compares average employment-to-population ratios by gender for Belgium, France, and Germany with Denmark, Sweden, and Norway in the year 2000.[3] The striking fact in this table is that while employment-to-population ratios are higher for both men and women in Scandinavia than in continental Europe, the difference between the two ratios for women is twice as large as the difference between the ratios for men. If, when family services are provided outside the market, it is typical for women to take on the much larger share of this type of work, then this finding is consistent with my earlier argument. By the same token, one would expect that if these services switched from being provided at home to being provided in the market, employment rates of women would increase.

TABLE 6-3

EMPLOYMENT-TO-POPULATION RATIOS BY GENDER, 2000

	Male	Female
Continental Europe	.70	.55
Scandinavia	.79	.73

SOURCE: OECD (http://stats.oecd.org/index.aspx?r=861732).
NOTES: Continental Europe = Belgium, France, Germany, and Italy. Scandinavia = Sweden, Denmark, and Norway.

In light of this discussion, it is also interesting to look at the time series behavior of the employment-to-population ratio for females across these two sets of countries and the United States. This is done in figure 6-3. The figure starts in 1963, since this is the first year that the data are available for Sweden.

FIGURE 6-3

FEMALE EMPLOYMENT-TO-POPULATION RATIOS, 1963–2000

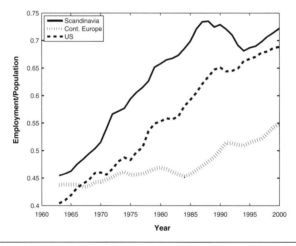

SOURCE: OECD (http://stats.oecd.org/index.aspx?r=861732).
NOTES: Continental Europe = Belgium, France, Germany, and Italy. Scandinavia = Sweden, Denmark, and Norway.

A few striking points can be noted. First, back in 1963 there is relatively little difference in female employment-to-population ratios, and to the extent that there is a difference, the United States has the lowest value. Chapter 4 commented on the rising employment-to-population ratio for women for the United States, so that feature is not new to us. Second, when we contrast the change in the employment-to-population ratio in the United States with that of continental Europe, we see that the U.S. ratio increases throughout the entire period, while the ratio in continental Europe is relatively flat for the first twenty or so years and then begins to rise. What is striking about this timing is that the large tax increases in continental Europe also coincide with the period prior to the mid-1980s, so that this figure shows that once taxes stopped increasing, female employment rates also started to exhibit the same rise that they have exhibited elsewhere. Earlier I argued that although the same underlying forces leading to greater female labor market participation are present in all advanced economies, increasing tax rates serve to offset this underlying force. The above figure shows that once taxes stopped increasing, the effects of the underlying force become evident.

Now, let's turn to the behavior of female employment in Scandinavia. Figure 6-3 shows that female employment exhibits an ongoing increase in Scandinavia just as in the United States, though the extent of the overall increase is somewhat lower in Scandinavia. This is consistent with the argument made above that at the same time that Scandinavia was increasing taxes on labor, it was simultaneously using these tax revenues in ways to increase the incentives for women to work in the market.

Summary

Scandinavia is not after all a sharp counterexample to the view that labor taxes have substantial disincentive effects. The messages of the basic theory laid out in chapter 1, combined with a close look at the overall package of labor taxes and government spending in these countries, suggest that Scandinavia is not inconsistent with my findings. There is still a need for more work on the exact details of Scandinavian policy and for an assessment of the precise quantitative effects of those policies. Such work would help us understand even better how and why the dynamics of taxes and hours of work in Scandinavia differ so much from those of continental Europe.

Conclusion

The issue that I set out to analyze in this monograph concerns the magnitude of the disincentive effects of labor taxes. There are two key messages that I want the reader of this monograph to take away. The first is cautionary in nature: one needs to be careful about asserting that taxes on labor necessarily or always lead to less work in the overall economy. It turns out that what the government does with tax revenues is a very relevant consideration. When the government uses the revenues either to fund transfer programs or to provide services such as education or health care free of charge, then higher taxes will cause individuals to work less.

The second and more important message is that the size of these disincentive effects is large. By examining the time series data for the United States and several OECD countries since 1960, I conclude that a 10 percent increase in the share of GDP devoted to transfer programs would lead to a decrease in aggregate hours of work in the economy of between 10 and 15 percent. To put this number in perspective, note that any decrease in hours worked of 3 percent or more relative to trend constitutes a large recession. So the magnitude of these effects is indeed very substantial.

A key concern of this book is where we should look for evidence of these disincentive effects. I have argued that these effects are present in the U.S. data, but that a problem with looking for them there is that the United States has not experienced changes in labor taxes that are large relative to other changes occurring at the same time. The ideal place to look for this information lies in the experiences of other advanced economies during the post-1960 period. The reason is that many of these countries have increased taxes by much more than the United States, in some cases by roughly three times as much. The response of hours of work to these large permanent changes in the scale of tax and transfer programs provides clear evidence of the magnitude of the effects that we are interested in.

In looking at this data I have relied on very simple methods. My belief is that when clearly presented, these data from other countries speak very loudly about the effect of higher labor taxes on work incentives. Since I have relied on a simple presentation of the data, as opposed to a more complicated and technical analysis, I emphasize that the estimates provided here are not the final word on the magnitude of the disincentive effects of taxes on labor. More detailed and sophisticated analyses of the experiences in other countries should yield more information; in particular, it is important to know if there are specific features of transfer programs which create larger disincentive effects. We would like to learn, for example, which aspects of the rules that govern the payments into Social Security and other federal benefit programs are most distortionary in terms of the labor supply decisions of individuals.[1] As I have stressed, it is also important to assess the potential benefits associated with various transfer programs in order to properly compare the programs' costs and benefits.

In the final pages of this study, I want to discuss some broad implications of the key findings for current policy discussions. I think it is well understood that the aging population and the increasing cost of health care are going to create the need for substantial additional revenues if the current structure of entitlement programs is not changed. Moreover, the Obama administration has made it clear that it plans to consider potentially far-reaching reforms in health care, Social Security, and education. One plain implication of this monograph is that any analyses of entitlement programs will need to consider how these programs influence work incentives.

There are two different ways in which taxes' effects on work matter. One concerns some very practical accounting issues involved in assessing government finances. An important calculation for a projected increase in government spending, or for measures to reduce the deficit while holding spending constant, is how much tax rates need to be increased in order to raise sufficient revenue. The larger are the disincentive effects of taxes, the larger is the required tax increase, since the decrease in work that accompanies the increase in taxes creates an opposing force. In other words, the larger the disincentive effects of taxation, the greater the tax increase that is required to finance a given increase in spending. It follows that the effects documented in this monograph have very direct implications for how future budget consequences are assessed. Simply put, future budget calculations that ignore the disincentive effects of higher tax rates on labor will seriously distort the accuracy of future budget forecasts. Moreover, given taxes' disincentive effects, there are very definite limits on how much revenue the government can raise by taxing labor.

The second concern about taxes' disincentive effects involves the economic costs of policies that discourage individuals from working and hence producing output. A simple example may help to illustrate these costs. Consider an economy in which everyone is spending $50 per month out of pocket for medication, and for now assume that everyone earns the same income from working. If the government were to tax labor income so as to raise $50 per month per person on average and then use this money to pay for everyone's out-of-pocket medication costs, there would appear to be no cost, since government is effectively taking $50 from each individual and then giving it back in the form of medication. But my analysis shows why this assessment is erroneous. If people know that they must pay $50 for their medication, then they know that they need to work to generate the $50 in income. But if the government pays $50 for everyone's medication, then people no longer need to generate income to buy the medication, and as a result the incentive to work is decreased. The analysis in this book argues that this disincentive effect is large.

In a more elaborate version of this example, different individuals have different labor incomes, so that if the government taxes everyone at the same rate in an attempt to raise the required revenues, some individuals will pay more than average in taxes and some individuals will pay less than average. In this case the government program also serves to redistribute income across individuals. But the same issue still arises: one of the implicit costs of this redistributive scheme is that work incentives are reduced. Different individuals may have different views on whether redistribution in this context is a good thing, but even if someone believes that this redistribution has important benefits, the disincentive effects on work are still a cost that needs to be taken into account. The simple but important conclusion from this example is that one needs to be especially wary of programs that essentially take money from people, pass it through the government, and return it to the taxpayers in the form of a transfer.

The fact that my example dealt with health care expenditures was no coincidence, since it is very much in this context that these types of transfer programs are becoming more and more prominent. One of the key choices that the United States will face in the future will be between increasing taxes to pay for Medicare or changing the program so that individuals pay higher user fees. The disincentive effects documented in this monograph suggest that there are important benefits associated with moving to a system with higher user fees.

The same argument can be made for education costs, especially those associated with higher education. It is important to distinguish between the government subsidizing education costs, say by lowering tuition, versus the government making sure that individuals have access to student loans in order to finance the cost of going to school. In the case of loans the student will eventually pay for the cost of the education; all the loan does is change the timing of the payments. In the case of subsidies, the disincentive effects will be felt.

Similar issues need to be addressed in the context of the Social Security system. Unless benefits are reduced or the full retirement age is increased, this program will require higher tax rates in the future. The disincentive effects associated with a program like this need to be a key issue in the debate about reforming Social Security.

The mere fact that the taxes required to finance government programs entail a disincentive effect does not imply that all government programs are a bad idea, or that the size of government should be minimized. Each program has its potential benefits in addition to these costs, and the ultimate assessment of any program must depend on a careful examination of these costs and benefits. But assessments that ignore the potentially large disincentive effects documented in this monograph will likely lead to a far greater expansion in government programs than is warranted. This message is particularly relevant today as a larger role for government is debated, and as decisions are made about the long-run size of government in the United States.

Appendix

This appendix provides a more rigorous derivation of the results that were presented in chapter 1. For expositional ease I will adopt one commonly used utility function that has the property that income and substitution effects offset one another. Specifically, I will assume that $u(c, 1 - h)$ is of the form

$$u(c, 1 - h) = \log(c) + v(1 - h),$$

where the function v is assumed to be increasing and concave. The technical assumption of concavity intuitively implies that as an individual increases his or her amount of leisure, the value of additional leisure decreases. That is, when an individual is working a lot and hence has very little leisure, an additional unit of leisure is very valuable, but when an individual is not working very much and already has a lot of leisure time, an additional unit of leisure is not as valuable. The utility that an individual gets from consumption also displays this same property: when consumption is low, the extra utility that is obtained from a small increase in consumption is very large, but when consumption is high, the extra utility from a small increase in consumption is much less.

Consider an individual with zero nonlabor income.[1] To see that this utility function has the property just referred to, we consider the problem that this individual faces in deciding his or her desired level of work. Formally, this problem can be written as

$$\max_{c,h} \log c + v(1 - h)$$
$$s.t. c = wh.$$

Substituting the budget equation into the objective function, one can rewrite this problem as

$$\max_h \log(wh) + v(1 - h).$$

Mathematically, this corresponds to the point at which the derivative of the objective function with respect to h is equal to zero, which happens when h satisfies the equation

$$\frac{1}{h} = v'(1 - h). \qquad (1)$$

Note that this equation does not contain w, which is to say that with this utility function, the desired level of labor supply is independent of the level of the wage.

Now let us move beyond the labor supply decision of a particular individual or household to analyze how the tax system in a given economy affects the time devoted to work in the economy as a whole. In order to apply the model to such a question, we will enlarge it along two dimensions. First, instead of assuming a single individual, we will assume that there are a large number of individuals, denoted by N. While we could easily assume that each of these individuals has a different utility function, our focus will be on economy-wide averages, and for this there is no harm in assuming that all individuals have the same utility function.

The second dimension along which we extend the model is to explicitly include the fact that the time individuals devote to work will lead to output being produced, which in turn will meet the consumption demands of individuals in the economy. We write the relationship between total output produced (Y) and total time devoted to work (H) by the relationship

$$Y = AH,$$

where A is a positive constant. This production relationship implies that total output is proportional to the total amount of time devoted to work—i.e., if total time devoted to work increases by 10 percent, then so does output, and conversely, if total time devoted to work decreases by 10 percent, then so does output. This production relationship emphasizes the simple reality that if an economy reduces the time that it devotes to work, then it also reduces the amount of output available for consumption. This specification assumes that labor is the only input into the production of output. If we assume, as is often done, that capital is also an input into pro-duction, we can still carry out this analysis. That is, we can make the model dynamic and allow for capital accumulation, though doing so produces no additional insights and, as noted before, the analysis becomes more involved.

We can now solve for the competitive equilibrium of this economy. This standard benchmark notion of equilibrium assumes that consumers maxi-mize utility taking prices as given, that firms maximize profits taking prices as given, and that prices are such that demand and supply are equal in all markets. Once again, one can easily generalize this to allow for many addi-tional features, but this is not necessary for the points that I want to make. If we normalize the price of consumption to equal 1 as above, then the pro-duction function dictates that the equilibrium wage rate will be equal to A. This represents the simple notion that wages and productivity are linked, a notion that is strongly supported by the data. All individuals will have desired labor supply h that satisfies equation (1), and all individuals will have consumption consistent with their budget equation, given their chosen hours of work and the wage rate. Aggregate hours of work are simply Nh.

As in the text, we consider a government that faces the budget constraint

$$N\tau wh = N(G_u + G_w + T),$$

which reduces to

$$\tau wh = G_u + G_w + T.$$

We now study the competitive equilibrium of this economy, and in particular focus on how changes in government policy will influence economy-wide outcomes. The labor supply decision of an individual in this setting that includes government policy is now altered. Specifically, we can write the utility maximization problem of each individual as

$$\max_{c,h} \log(c + G_u) + v(1 - h)$$
$$s.t. c = (1 - \tau)wh + T.$$

It is important to note how government policy enters into this problem. The total consumption of an individual is given by the sum of private expenditure on consumption plus the useful goods and services provided by the government. The transfer payment shows up as a source of income on the right-hand side of the budget equation. Wasteful government spending does not directly enter this equation, since by definition it provides nothing of value to the individual.

Proceeding as before, we can use the budget equation to solve for c and substitute it into the objective function so that the problem can be written as

$$\max_h \log[(1 - \tau) wh + T + G_u] + v(1 - h).$$

As before, the optimal choice of h for this individual occurs at the point where the derivative of this function is equal to zero. This implies that

$$\frac{(1 - \tau)w}{(1 - \tau) wh + G_u + T} = v'(1 - h). \qquad (2)$$

This expression leads to several interesting results. First, consider the case where there are no transfer payments and there is no useful government spending, i.e., $T=0$ and $G_u=0$. Then the above expression reduces to

$$\frac{1}{h} = v'(1 - h),$$

which is the same as in equation (1). That is, if there are no transfer payments or useful government spending, then the tax rate on labor income has no effect on desired hours of work.

Next we consider the case in which there is no wasteful government spending, so that all spending takes the form of either transfer payments or useful government spending. The fact that the government budget is balanced requires that

$$\tau wh = T + G_u,$$

i.e., that on average, the amount each individual receives from the government equals the amount in taxes each individual pays to the government. Substituting this into equation (2) we obtain

$$\frac{(1-\tau)}{h} = v'(1 - h).$$

This equation implies that an increase in τ leads to a decrease in h. That is, an increase in the tax rate on labor income that is used to finance a transfer payment (or useful government spending) leads to a decrease in hours of work.

Generalizing from the earlier analysis, we now consider three different proportional taxes: a labor income tax levied on workers, denoted by τ_h, a consumption tax levied on consumers, denoted by τ_c, and a payroll tax levied on firms, denoted by τ_p. The budget equation for an individual now reads

$$(1 + \tau_c) c = (1 - \tau_h) wh + T.$$

To simplify exposition, assume now that the government uses its revenues entirely to finance transfer payments. The government budget constraint now reads

$$\tau_c c + \tau_h wh + \tau_p wh = T,$$

where the left-hand side is simply the sum of tax revenues from consumption taxes, labor income taxes, and payroll taxes, respectively. In the earlier analysis, the value of the wage in equilibrium was equal to A. A higher wage than A would lead to excess supply of labor, since firms would not find it profitable to hire workers; and a lower wage would lead to excess demand for labor, since firms would want to hire more and more workers. In the earlier analysis, the cost of labor to the firm was simply equal to the wage. If there is a payroll tax levied on firms, then the cost of labor to the firm is given by $w(1+\tau_p)$, so that in order for the labor market to be in equilibrium, the cost of labor must be equal to A, the marginal product of labor. That is, the equilibrium wage must now satisfy

$$w = \frac{A}{1 + \tau_p}.$$

Proceeding as before, the individual's optimal choice of h is derived from solving the following problem:

$$\max_h \log \left(\frac{(1 - \tau_h) wh + T}{1 + \tau_c} \right) + v(1 - h).$$

The condition that characterizes the optimal value of h is found by requiring that the derivative of this expression with respect to h be equal to zero, and gives

$$\frac{(1 - \tau_h)w}{(1 - \tau_h)wh + T} = v'(1 - h).$$

We have argued above that in equilibrium, $w = A/(1 + \tau_p)$. The denominator is equal to total income per worker. In equilibrium, all of this income is used to purchase consumption, so this must equal the amount of per-worker consumption produced divided by the price of consumption. The amount of consumption produced per worker is equal to Ah, and the price of consumption, including taxes, is equal to $(1+\tau_c)$. Making these substitutions gives us

$$\frac{(1 - \tau_h)}{(1 + \tau_c)(1 + \tau_p)h} = v'(1 - h).$$

If we define the effective tax on labor, denoted by τ, as

$$(1 - \tau)= \frac{(1 - \tau_h)}{(1 + \tau_c)(1 + \tau_p)}, \tag{3}$$

we see that the case with all three taxes is equivalent to a case in which there is only a tax on labor income equal to τ.

The natural way to introduce defense spending into the model is to assume that individuals have preferences given by

$$\log(c) + v(1 - h) + f(G_d),$$

where G_d denotes spending on defense and f is an increasing function. I will not go through the details, but it turns out that if the government taxes labor income to finance this type of spending, then, just as in the case of wasteful spending, there will be no effect on labor supply.

Notes

Introduction

1. The thirty member countries of the OECD include the richest countries in North America, Europe, and Asia and are typically identified as the most advanced economies in the world. All statistics in this paragraph come from the OECD.

Chapter 1: Labor Taxes and Hours of Work: Some Theory

1. Expressed formally, the individual makes his or her decision about how much to work so as to maximize utility $u(c,1-h)$ subject to the budget constraint $pc=wh+I$. The budget equation describes the different combinations of leisure and consumption that the individual can afford. It is apparent that what matters are the ratios w/p and I/p, and not the specific values of w, I, and p. That is, if we were to double the values of p, I, and w, then the individual would be in exactly the same situation in terms of his or her ability to generate consumption from working. The value w/p is known as the real wage, since it gives the amount of consumption that an individual can obtain per unit of time devoted to work, and I/p is the real value of nonlabor income.

2. Formally, the budget constraint for the government can be written as $N\tau wh=N(G_u+G_w+T)$, which reduces to $\tau wh=G_u+G_w+T$.

3. See also Rogerson (2006, 2007) for a more rigorous treatment.

4. If there were many different consumption goods and the government was providing much more of a particular good than individuals liked to consume, then this result would be affected. The government does not seem to be doing this for large expenditure items such as education and health care.

5. An important practical issue here concerns whether the government does as good a job providing goods or services as private providers. If not, then we would model the inefficiencies associated with government provision as reflecting a component of what we call wasteful spending. So, for example, if the government is spending $100 per person in providing some service that the individual could purchase from a private provider for $75, we would say that useful spending is $75 per person and wasteful spending is $25 per person.

6. It is worth noting that this result is true for any utility function as long as both consumption and leisure are assumed to be what economists call "normal goods," which means that a person with higher wealth would choose to consume more of each of them.

7. There is a long literature on the empirical analysis of the Laffer curve. See Trabandt and Uhlig (2006) for a recent examination and further references.

8. The exact relation is given by $(1-\tau)=(1-\tau_h)/[(1+\tau_c)(1+\tau_p)]$.

9. If s is the subsidy per unit offered by the government, then the budget equation for an individual can be written as $(1-s)pc=(1-\tau)wh+I+T$. It is important to note that the subsidy is per unit and not a given amount of money, i.e., the total amount of subsidy that individuals receive is dependent on how much consumption they choose to purchase.

Chapter 2: Labor Taxes and Hours of Work: Where to Look for Evidence?

1. See also Chang and Kim (2006) and Prescott, Rogerson, and Wallenius (2009) for additional analysis of this issue.

2. See McGrattan and Prescott (2009) for a theory that can account for the behavior of the U.S. economy in the 1990s.

3. The issue of how temporary changes in labor taxes and government spending influence hours of work is also an important one, and one that is very much in the news in the context of policy responses to the current recession. But it is not the focus of this monograph.

4. Davis and Henrekson (2004) also note the importance of looking for episodes of tax increases where sufficient time has elapsed to allow for individuals to fully respond.

Chapter 4: What We Learn from the U.S. Experience

1. Galor and Weil (1996), Goldin and Katz (2002), Greenwood, Seshadri, and Yorokoglu (2005), and Olivetti (2006) argue that it is different aspects of technological change that are important. Fernandez, Fogli, and Olivetti (2004) suggest that it is changing social norms. Jones, Manuelli, and McGrattan (2003) find that changes in discrimination are most important, and Attanasio, Low, and Sanchez-Marcos (2008) argue that changing costs of child care have played a key role.

2. On home production see also the survey article of Gronau (1986). Applications of home production to aggregate labor market outcomes include Benhabib, Rogerson, and Wright (1991), McGrattan, Rogerson and Wright.(1997), Rios-Rull (1993), Chang (2000), Ragan (2005), Rogerson (2007), McDaniel (2008), and Rogerson (2008).

3. Formally we would write $g(c,h_n)=[ac^\eta+(1-a)h_n^\eta]^{1/\eta}$, where the parameter η determines the elasticity of substitution between c and h_n.

4. Estimates from aggregate data are presented in McGrattan, Rogerson, and Wright (1997) and Chang and Schorfheide (2003), while estimates from microdata are in Rupert, Rogerson, and Wright (1995), and Aguiar and Hurst (2007b).

5. I have tried to keep the discussion at a nontechnical level. For the reader who would like to see a more formal analysis, both Rogerson (2008) and McDaniel (2008) present analyses of long-term changes in hours worked in the United States in the presence of changes in taxes and of a second force that leads to a reallocation of time from home production to market work.

Chapter 5: What We Learn from the Experience of Other Countries

1. Once again, I have tried to keep the presentation at a nontechnical level. The reader interested in a more structured analysis of these data in the context of a formal model of labor supply is referred to Ohanian, Raffo, and Rogerson (2008). See also Prescott (2004), Rogerson (2006, 2008), Pissarides (2007), McDaniel (2008), and Kitao, Ljungqvist, and Sargent (2008).

2. Or alternatively, as women engage in more market work there is an incentive for other household members (primarily husbands) to do less market work in order to assist with home production.

3. Excluding Sweden, the correlation coefficient is –0.50. The next chapter discusses why Sweden should be viewed differently.

4. The earlier tables in this chapter did not include New Zealand, since data limitations prevented McDaniel (2006) from computing tax rates for this country. But the data for hours worked are available for New Zealand from the same source as is used for the other countries, and they show New Zealand has hours of work comparable to those of Australia, Canada, and the United States.

5. The data to support this claim come from Alesina, Glaeser, and Sacerdote (2005).

6. Alesina, Glaeser, and Sacerdote (2005) present data from another source which challenge this conclusion. These authors note, however, their data set seems ill suited to cross-country comparisons. The Harmonised European Time Use data set used by Ragan (2005) was designed to specifically address the shortcomings mentioned by Alesina and others and hence seems more reliable.

7. In comparing countries using the 2003 data, it is important to recall the changes in the U.S. survey design mentioned in chapter 4: relative to earlier surveys in the United States, the American Time Use Survey, initiated as part of the Current Population Survey, tends to generate larger amounts of time reported to child care. In the United States this results in an almost 50 percent increase in time devoted to child care relative to the 1985 time-use survey data.

Chapter 6: Understanding Scandinavia

1. *OECD Historical Statistics* (Paris: OECD Publishing), 1995.

2. Ibid.

3. I do not include Italy in this comparison. The Mediterranean economies of Spain, Italy, and Greece all have substantially lower rates of female employment than other European economies, which many attribute to cultural differences.

4. Note that in this discussion the continental European average is only for three countries: Belgium, France, and Germany. Female employment in Italy is substantially lower than in these countries. I wanted to be clear that Italy was not the driving force behind any comparisons, and so to emphasize this I have left Italy out of the comparison.

5. One step in this direction has been taken by Ragan (2005) and Rogerson (2007), both of whom use the type of model talked about in chapter 4 to assess some aspects of Scandinavian tax and spending programs.

Conclusion

1. Ljungqvist and Sargent (2006) emphasize the need to explicitly model the details of benefit programs.

Appendix

1. The analysis also applies to a case in which there is nonlabor income, if we assume that nonlabor income has grown at the same rate as labor income over the last fifty years. This assumption is a good description of the actual data.

References

Aguiar, M., and E. Hurst. 2007a. Measuring leisure: The allocation of time over five decades. *Quarterly Journal of Economics* 122: 969–1006.

———. 2007b. Life cycle prices and consumption. *American Economic Review* 97: 1533–59.

Alesina, A., E. Glaeser, and B. Sacerdote. 2005. Work and leisure in the U.S. and Europe: Why so different? In *NBER macroeconomics annual*, ed. Mark Gertler and Kenneth Rogoff, 1–64. Cambridge, MA: MIT Press.

Attanasio, O., H. Low, and V. Sanchez-Marcos. 2008. Explaining changes in female labor supply in a life cycle model. *American Economic Review* 98: 1517–52.

Becker, Gary. 1965. A theory of the allocation of time. *Economic Journal* 75: 493–517.

Benhabib, J., R. Rogerson, and R. Wright. 1991. Homework in macroeconomics: Household production and aggregate fluctuations. *Journal of Political Economy* 99 (1991): 1166–87.

Burda, Michael, Dan Hamermesh, and Philippe Weil. 2008. The distribution of total work in the EU and U.S. In *Are Europeans lazy? or Americans crazy?* ed. Tito Boeri, 11–100. Oxford: Oxford University Press.

Chang, Y. 2000. Comovement, excess volatility and home production. *Journal of Monetary Economics* 46: 385–96.

———, and S. Kim. 2006. From individual to aggregate labor supply: A quantitative analysis based on a heterogeneous-agent macroeconomy. *International Economic Review* 47: 1–27.

Chang, Y., and F. Schorfheide. 2003. Labor supply shifts and economic fluctuations. *Journal of Monetary Economics* 50: 1751–68.

Davis, S., and M. Henrekson. 2004. Tax effects on work activity, industry mix and shadow economy size: Evidence from rich country comparisons. NBER Working Paper no. 10509.

Fernandez, R., A. Fogli, and C. Olivetti. 2004. Mothers and sons: Preference transmission and female labor force dynamics. *Quarterly Journal of Economics* 119: 1249–99.

Francis, N., and V. Ramey. 2009. A century of work and leisure. *American Economic Journal: Macroeconomics* 1: 189–224.

Freeman, R., and R. Schettkat. 2001. Marketization of production and the U.S.-Europe employment gap. *Oxford Bulletin of Economics and Statistics* 63: 647–70.

———. 2005. Marketization of household production and the EU-US gap in work. *Economic Policy* 20: 6–50.

Galor, O., and D. Weil. 1996. The gender gap, fertility, and growth. *American Economic Review* 86: 374–87.

Goldin, C., and L. Katz. 2002. The power of the pill: Oral contraceptives and women's career and marriage decisions. *Journal of Political Economy* 110: 730–70.

Greenwood, J., A. Seshadri, and M. Yorokoglu. 2005. Engines of liberation. *Review of Economic Studies* 72: 109–33.

Gronau, R. 1986. Home production: A survey. In *Handbook of labor economics*, ed. O. Ashenfelter and R. Layard, 273–304. Amsterdam: Elsevier Science, 1986.

Imai, S., and M. Keane. 2004. Intertemporal labor supply and human capital accumulation. *International Economic Review* 45: 601–41.

Joines, D. 1981. Estimates of effective marginal tax rates on factor incomes. *Journal of Business* 54: 191–226.

Jones, L., R. Manuelli, and E. McGrattan. 2003. Why are married women working so much? Federal Reserve Bank of Minneapolis Staff Report 317.

Kitao, S., L. Ljungqvist, and T. Sargent. 2008. A life cycle model of transatlantic employment experiences. Available at http://sites.google.com/site/sagirikitao/research3.

Ljungqvist, L., and T. Sargent. 2006. Do taxes explain European employment? Indivisible labor, human capital, lotteries and savings. In *NBER macroeconomics annual*, ed. Daron Acemoglu, Kenneth Rogoff, and Michael Woodford, 181–224. Cambridge, MA: MIT Press

MaCurdy, T. 1981. An empirical model of labor supply in a life cycle setting. *Journal of Political Economy* 89: 1059–85.

McDaniel, C. 2006. Effective tax rates for 15 OECD countries: 1950–2003. Manuscript, Arizona State University, Department of Economics.

———. 2008. Hours of work in the OECD 1960–2003: Driving forces and propagation mechanisms. Manuscript, Arizona State University, Department of Economics.

McGrattan, E. R., and E. Prescott. 2009. Unmeasured investment and the puzzling U.S. boom in the 1990s. Federal Reserve Bank of Minneapolis Staff Report no. 369.

McGrattan, E. R., R. Rogerson, and R. Wright. 1997. An equilibrium model of the business cycle with household production and fiscal policy. *International Economic Review* 38: 267–90.

Mendoza, E., A. Razin, and L. Tesar. 1994. Effective tax rates in macroeconomics: Cross-country estimates of tax rates on factor incomes and consumption. *Journal of Monetary Economics* 34: 297–323.

Ohanian, L., A. Raffo, and R. Rogerson, 2008. Long-term changes in labor supply and taxes: Evidence from OECD countries, 1956–2004. *Journal of Monetary Economics* 55: 1353–62.

Olivetti, C. 2006. Changes in women's hours of market work: The role of returns to experience. *Review of Economic Dynamics* 9: 557–87.

Pissarides, C. 2007. Unemployment and hours of work: The North Atlantic divide revisited. *International Economic Review* 48 (February): 1–36.

Prescott, E. 2004. Why do Americans work so much more than Europeans? *Quarterly Review of the Federal Reserve Bank of Minneapolis* (July): 2–13.

Prescott, E., Rogerson, R., and Wallenius, J. 2009. Lifetime aggregate labor supply with endogenous workweek length. *Review of Economic Dynamics* 12: 23–36.

Ragan, K. 2005. Fiscal policy and the family: Explaining labor supply in a model with household production. Working paper, University of Chicago, Department of Economics.

Rios-Rull, J. 1993. Working in the market, working at home and the acquisition of skills: A general equilibrium approach. *American Economic Review* 83: 893–907.

Rogerson, R. 2006. Understanding differences in hours worked. *Review of Economic Dynamics* 9: 365–409.

———. 2007. Taxes and market work: Is Scandinavia an outlier? *Economic Theory* 32: 59–85.

———. 2008. Structural transformation and the deterioration of European labor market outcomes. *Journal of Political Economy* 116: 235–59.

———, and J. Wallenius. 2009. Micro and macro elasticities in a life cycle model with taxes. *Journal of Economic Theory* 144: 2277–92.

Rupert, P., R. Rogerson, and R. Wright. 1995. Estimating substitution elasticities in household production models. *Economic Theory* 6: 179–93.

Trabandt, M., and H. Uhlig. 2006. How far are we from the slippery slope? The Laffer curve revisited. SFB 649 Discussion Paper 2006-03, http://sfb649.wiwi.hu-berlin.de/papers/pdf/SFB649DP2006-023.pdf.

About the Author

Richard Rogerson is Rondthaler Professor of Economics and Regents' Professor at the W. P. Carey School of Business at Arizona State University. Prior to joining the faculty at ASU, he was a professor of economics at the University of Pennsylvania from 1997 to 2001. Since receiving his Ph.D. in Economics from the University of Minnesota in 1984, he has also held faculty positions at the University of Rochester, New York University, Stanford University, and the University of Minnesota. Dr. Rogerson's teaching and research interests are in the fields of labor economics and macroeconomics. His published work includes papers on labor supply and taxes, business cycle fluctuations, the effects of labor market regulations, financing of public education, and development. Dr. Rogerson currently serves as associate editor of the *Review of Economic Dynamics* and is a member of the editorial board of the *American Economic Journal: Macroeconomics*. He previously served as co-editor of the *American Economic Review* and associate editor of the *Journal of Monetary Economics*, the *Journal of Economic Dynamics,* and *Control and the International Economic Review*. He is a research associate at the National Bureau of Economic Research and a fellow of the Econometric Society.